Employers are responsible for providing a safe and healthful workplace for their employees. OSHA's role is to assure the safety and health of America's employees by setting and enforcing standards; providing training, outreach and education; establishing partnerships; and encouraging continual improvement in workplace safety and health.

This handbook provides a general overview of a particular topic related to OSHA standards. It does not alter or determine compliance responsibilities in OSHA standards or the *Occupational Safety and Health Act of 1970*. Because interpretations and enforcement policy may change over time, you should consult current OSHA administrative interpretations and decisions by the Occupational Safety and Health Review Commission and the Courts for additional guidance on OSHA compliance requirements.

This information is available to sensory impaired individuals upon request. Voice phone: (202) 693-1999; teletypewriter (TTY) number: (877) 889-5627.

Small Entity Compliance Guide
for the
Hexavalent Chromium Standards

Occupational Safety and Health Administration
U.S. Department of Labor

OSHA 3320-10N
2006

Contents

Introduction   3

Scope   4

Definitions   5

Permissible Exposure Limit (PEL)   6

Exposure Determination   7

Regulated Areas   9

Methods of Compliance   9

Respiratory Protection   11

Protective Work Clothing
and Equipment   11

Hygiene Areas and Practices   13

Housekeeping   14

Medical Surveillance   15

Communication of Cr(VI) Hazards
to Employees   16

Recordkeeping   17

Dates   18

OSHA Assistance   19

Appendix I:
OSHA Cr(VI) Standards   22

Appendix II:
Industry Operations or Processes
Associated with Occupational
Exposure to Cr(VI)   40

Appendix III:
A. OSHA Area Offices   47

B. OSHA Regional Offices   52

C. States with Approved Occupational
   Safety and Health Plans   53

D. OSHA Consultation Project
   Directory   55

Cover photo: An employee welds a stainless steel flange using a tungsten inert gas (TIG) welding process (courtesy Bath Iron Works).

**Occupational Safety and
Health Administration**

Introduction

This guide is intended to help small businesses comply with the Occupational Safety and Health Administration's (OSHA) Hexavalent Chromium (Cr(VI)) standards. Employees exposed to Cr(VI) are at increased risk of developing serious adverse health effects including lung cancer, asthma and damage to the nasal passages and skin. This guide describes the steps that employers are required to take to protect employees from the hazards associated with exposure to Cr(VI).

This document provides guidance only, and does not alter or determine compliance responsibilities, which are set forth in OSHA standards and the *Occupational Safety and Health Act*. This guide does not replace the official Hexavalent Chromium standards, which are contained in Appendix I of this document. The employer must refer to the appropriate standard to ensure that they are in compliance. Moreover, because interpretations and enforcement policy may change over time, for additional guidance on OSHA compliance requirements the reader should consult current administrative interpretations and decisions by the Occupational Safety and Health Review Commission and the courts.

In 24 states and two territories, OSHA standards are enforced by the state agency responsible for the OSHA-approved State Plan. These states and territories are: Alaska, Arizona, California, Connecticut, Hawaii, Indiana, Iowa, Kentucky, Maryland, Michigan, Minnesota, Nevada, New Jersey, New Mexico, New York, North Carolina, Oregon, Puerto Rico, South Carolina, Tennessee, Utah, Vermont, Virgin Islands, Virginia, Washington, and Wyoming. Connecticut, New Jersey, New York, and the Virgin Islands operate OSHA-approved State Plans limited in scope to state and local government employees. State Plans must adopt and enforce standards that are either identical to or at least as effective as the federal standards. They must also extend the coverage of their standards to state and local government employees.

HOW TO USE THIS GUIDE

The guide is divided into sections that correspond to the major provisions of the Cr(VI) standards. Each section follows the same organization as the corresponding paragraph of the standards, providing more detail than the standards to help employers better understand the requirements. For example, the Scope section explains which employers are covered by the standards and describes the exceptions to coverage of the standards. The employer may consult a section that is of particular interest, or may proceed through the sections in sequence to gain a better understanding of the standards in their entirety. A section describing additional OSHA resources available to assist employers is also included.

The Cr(VI) standards for general industry (29 CFR 1910.1026), shipyards (29 CFR 1915.1026), and construction (29 CFR 1926.1126) are included in Appendix I. Appendix II presents information on industry operations and processes associated with exposure to Cr(VI) to assist employers in identifying Cr(VI) exposures in their workplaces. Appendix III contains listings of OSHA Area and Regional offices; the addresses and phone numbers of state agencies that administer OSHA-approved State Plans; and the addresses and phone numbers of OSHA Consultation Service offices.

WHERE TO GO FOR ADDITIONAL ASSISTANCE

For additional assistance in complying with the Cr(VI) standards, contact the nearest OSHA Area Office. If you are unable to contact the OSHA Area Office, you can contact the appropriate OSHA Regional Office for information or assistance. If you are located in a state that operates an OSHA-approved State Plan, you may contact the responsible state agency for information and assistance. See Appendix III for the addresses and phone numbers of these offices.

The OSHA Consultation Service is another important resource for additional assistance. The service is largely funded by OSHA and is delivered by state governments using well-trained professional staff. Primarily intended for smaller businesses, the consultation program is free of charge to employers and is completely separate from the OSHA inspection effort. The consultation services do not issue citations or propose penalties. Additional information on the OSHA Consultation Service, as well as other sources of help from OSHA, can be found in the OSHA assistance section of the guide.

The standards apply to all occupational exposures to Cr(VI), with only limited exceptions. OSHA has separate standards for Cr(VI) exposures in general industry, shipyards, and construction. Most of the requirements are the same for all sectors. Where there are differences, they will be explained in this guide.

Cr(VI) is present in many different compounds that have a variety of industrial applications. Examples of major industrial uses of Cr(VI) compounds include: chromate pigments in dyes, paints, inks, and plastics; chromates added as anticorrosive agents to paints, primers, and other surface coatings; and chromic acid electroplated onto metal parts to provide a decorative or protective coating. Examples of Cr(VI) compounds include:

- ammonium dichromate ($(NH_4)_2Cr_2O_7$);
- calcium chromate ($CaCrO_4$);
- chromium trioxide or chromic acid (CrO_3);
- lead chromate ($PbCrO_4$);
- potassium chromate (K_2CrO_4);
- potassium dichromate ($K_2Cr_2O_7$);
- sodium chromate (Na_2CrO_4);
- strontium chromate ($SrCrO_4$); and
- zinc chromate ($ZnCrO_4$).

Employers can consult their suppliers or examine material safety data sheets (MSDSs) to identify Cr(VI)-containing materials that are present in the workplace.

Cr(VI) can also be formed when performing "hot work" such as welding on stainless steel, melting chromium metal, or heating refractory bricks in kilns. In these situations the chromium is not originally hexavalent, but the high temperatures involved in the process result in oxidation that converts the chromium to a hexavalent state. Appendix II of this document presents a more extensive description of the industry operations and processes that are typically associated with Cr(VI) exposure.

The Cr(VI) standards do not apply in three situations: Exposures that occur in the application of pesticides; exposures to portland cement; and where the employer has objective data demonstrating that Cr(VI) concentrations cannot exceed 0.5 micrograms per cubic meter of air as an 8-hour time-weighted average under any expected conditions of use.

APPLICATION OF PESTICIDES

The standards do not cover exposures to Cr(VI) that occur in the application of pesticides. Some Cr(VI)-containing chemicals, such as chromated copper arsenate (CCA) and acid copper chromate (ACC), are used for wood treatment and are regulated by the Environmental Protection Agency (EPA) as pesticides. OSHA does not regulate where another federal agency, such as EPA, enforces occupational safety and health standards.

The exemption pertains only to the application of pesticides and not to the manufacture of Cr(VI)-containing pesticides, which is covered by the standards. The use of wood treated with pesticides containing Cr(VI) is also covered by the standards.

PORTLAND CEMENT

The standards do not cover exposure to Cr(VI) in portland cement. Trace amounts of Cr(VI) are usually present in portland cement. However, the concentration of Cr(VI) is so low that employee exposures to Cr(VI) from working with portland cement are typically well below the action level.

Employers should be aware that other standards are in place to protect employees exposed to portland cement. OSHA has a permissible exposure limit for portland cement (see 29 CFR 1910.1000 for general industry; 29 CFR 1915.1000 for shipyards; 29 CFR 1926.55 for construction). Appropriate personal protective equipment must be provided and used when working with portland cement (see 29 CFR 1910.132 for general industry; 29 CFR 1915.152 for shipyards; 29 CFR 1926.95 for construction). Adequate washing facilities must also be provided in all sectors (see 29 CFR 1910.141(d) for general industry and shipyards; 29 CFR 1926.51(f) for construction). In addition, OSHA's Hazard Communication standard (29 CFR 1910.1200) requires training for all employees potentially exposed to hazardous chemicals, including portland cement.

WHERE EXPOSURES CANNOT EXCEED 0.5 µg/m³

An exemption from the standards is provided for employers who have objective data demonstrating that a material containing chromium or a specific process, operation, or activity involving chromium cannot release dusts, fumes, or mists of Cr(VI) in concentrations at or above 0.5 micrograms per cubic meter of air (0.5 µg/m³) as an 8-hour time-weighted average (TWA) under any expected conditions of use. When using the phrase "any expected conditions of use," OSHA is referring to any situation that can reasonably be foreseen by the employer. The meaning of the term "objective data" is discussed in the following section.

This exception for situations where exposures are not likely to present significant risk to employees allows employers to focus their resources on exposures of greater occupational health concern.

OSHA
Occupational Safety and
Health Administration

Definitions are included in the standards to describe the meaning of a number of terms used. Some of these terms are further explained as follows:

Action level is defined as an airborne concentration of 2.5 micrograms of Cr(VI) per cubic meter of air (2.5 $\mu g/m^3$) calculated as an 8-hour time-weighted average (TWA) (i.e., employee exposures to Cr(VI) average 2.5 $\mu g/m^3$ over an eight-hour time period). Exposures at or above the action level trigger certain requirements for exposure monitoring and medical surveillance.

Chromium (VI) [Hexavalent chromium or Cr(VI)] means chromium with a valence of positive six, in any form or chemical compound in which it occurs. This term includes Cr(VI) in all states of matter, in any solution or other mixture, even if it is encapsulated by another substance. The term also includes Cr(VI) when it is created by an industrial process, such as when welding on stainless steel generates Cr(VI) fume.

Emergency means any occurrence that results, or is likely to result, in an uncontrolled release of Cr(VI). Such an occurrence may be the result of equipment failure, rupture of containers, or failure of control equipment. To constitute an emergency, the exposure must be unexpected and significant. If an incidental release of Cr(VI) can be controlled at the time of the release by employees in the immediate release area, or by maintenance personnel, it is not considered an emergency. For example, a minor spill that can be cleaned up by an employee with minimal airborne or dermal exposure to Cr(VI) would not be considered an emergency. Instances that do constitute an emergency trigger requirements for medical surveillance and the use of respiratory protection.

Employee exposure means exposure to Cr(VI) that would occur if the employee were not using a respirator. Thus, exposure levels should be determined outside of the respirator for those employees wearing a respirator.

Historical monitoring data is data from Cr(VI) exposure monitoring conducted prior to May 30, 2006 (the effective date of this Cr(VI) standard). In order for an employer to rely upon historical data, the data must

have been obtained during work operations conducted under workplace conditions that closely resemble the processes, types of material, control methods, work practices, and environmental conditions in the employer's current operations. Historical monitoring data must also comply with confidence and accuracy requirements specified in the exposure determination section of the standard.

Objective data means information, other than employee monitoring, that demonstrates the expected employee exposure to Cr(VI) associated with a particular product or material or a specific process, operation, or activity. Information that can serve as objective data includes, but is not limited to, air monitoring data from industry-wide surveys; data collected by a trade association from its members; or calculations based on the composition or chemical and physical properties of a material. Use of objective data is discussed in the exposure determination section under the "performance-oriented" option.

Physician or other licensed health care professional [PLHCP] is an individual whose legally permitted scope of practice (i.e., license, registration, or certification) allows him or her to independently provide or be delegated the responsibility to provide some or all of the particular health care services required by the medical surveillance provisions of this standard.

Regulated area means an area, demarcated by the employer, where an employee's exposure to airborne concentrations of Cr(VI) exceeds, or can reasonably be expected to exceed, the PEL. The employer has the responsibility to determine and demarcate the boundaries of the regulated area. OSHA has not included requirements for regulated areas in construction or shipyard workplaces.

The standards establish an 8-hour time-weighted average exposure limit of 5 micrograms of Cr(VI) per cubic meter of air (5 µg/m³). This means that over the course of any 8-hour work shift, the average exposure to Cr(VI) cannot exceed 5 µg/m³.

Calculation of Time-Weighted Average Exposures

Both the PEL and the action level are expressed as time-weighted average (TWA) exposures. TWA measurements account for variable exposure levels over the course of a work shift, averaging periods of higher and lower exposures. The TWA exposure for an 8-hour work shift is computed using a simple formula:

$$TWA = (C_a T_a + C_b T_b + \ldots C_n T_n) \div 8$$

Where:

TWA is the time-weighted average exposure for the work shift;

C is the concentration during any period of time (T) where the concentration remains constant; and

T is the duration in hours of the exposure at the concentration (C).

For example, assume that an employee is subject to the following exposure to Cr(VI):

Two hours exposure at 10 µg/m³
Two hours exposure at 5 µg/m³
Four hours exposure at 1 µg/m³

Substituting this information in the formula, we have:

$$(2 \times 10 + 2 \times 5 + 4 \times 1) \div 8 = 4.25 \ \mu g/m^3$$

Since 4.25 µg/m³ is more than 2.5 µg/m³, the action level has been exceeded. However, as 4.25 µg/m³ is less than 5 µg/m³, the PEL has not been exceeded.

OSHA
**Occupational Safety and
Health Administration**

Exposure Determination

Employers must determine the 8-hour time-weighted average exposure to Cr(VI) for each employee exposed to Cr(VI). This assessment allows the employer to identify and prevent overexposures; collect exposure data so that proper control methods can be selected; and evaluate the effectiveness of those methods. An accurate exposure determination also provides important information concerning occupational Cr(VI) exposures to the physician or other licensed health care professional who performs medical examinations on employees. Employers can choose between two options for performing exposure determinations: a scheduled monitoring option, or a performance-oriented option. In addition, employers must comply with certain requirements regarding employee notification of the results of the exposure determination, accuracy of measurement methods, and observation of monitoring.

SCHEDULED MONITORING OPTION

Employers who select the scheduled monitoring option must conduct initial exposure monitoring to determine employee exposure to Cr(VI). This monitoring is performed by sampling the air within the employee's breathing zone. Monitoring must represent the employee's time-weighted average exposure to airborne Cr(VI) over an 8-hour workday.

Employers must accurately characterize the exposure to Cr(VI) for each employee. In some cases, this will entail monitoring all exposed employees. In other cases, monitoring "representative" employees is sufficient. Representative exposure sampling is permitted when a number of employees perform essentially the same job under the same conditions. For such situations, it may be sufficient to monitor a fraction of these employees in order to obtain data that are "representative" of the remaining employees. Representative personal sampling for employees engaged in similar work involving similar Cr(VI) exposures is achieved by monitoring the employee(s) reasonably expected to have the highest Cr(VI) exposures. For example, this may involve monitoring the Cr(VI) exposure of the employee closest to an exposure source. This exposure result may then be attributed to the remaining employees in the group. Monitoring must accurately characterize exposures on each shift, for each job classification, and in each work area.

Requirements for periodic monitoring depend on the results of initial monitoring. If the initial monitoring indicates that employee exposures are below the action level, no further monitoring is required unless changes in the workplace may result in new or additional exposures. If the initial monitoring reveals employee exposures to be at or above the action level but at or below the PEL, the employer must perform periodic monitoring at least every six months. If the initial monitoring reveals employee exposures to be above the PEL, the employer must perform periodic monitoring at least every three months.

If periodic monitoring results indicate that employee exposures have fallen below the action level, and those results are confirmed by consecutive measurements taken at least seven days apart, the employer may discontinue monitoring for those employees whose exposures are represented by such monitoring. Similarly, after initial monitoring shows exposures above the PEL, if periodic measurements indicate that exposures are at or below the PEL but are at or above the action level, the employer may reduce the frequency of the monitoring to at least every six months.

Employers must perform additional monitoring when workplace changes may result in new or additional exposures to Cr(VI). These changes include alterations in the production process, raw materials, equipment, personnel, work practices, or control methods used in the workplace. For example, if an employer has conducted monitoring for an electroplating operation while using fume suppressants, and the use of fume suppressants is discontinued, then additional monitoring would be necessary to determine employee exposures under the modified conditions. In addition, there may be other situations which can result in new or additional exposures to Cr(VI) which are unique to an employer's work situation. For instance, a welder may move from an open, outdoor location to an enclosed or confined space. Even though the task performed and materials used may remain constant, the changed environment could reasonably be expected to result in higher exposures to Cr(VI). In these special situations, OSHA requires the employer to perform additional monitoring whenever the employer has any reason to believe that a change has occurred which may result in new or additional exposures to Cr(VI). Additional monitoring is not required simply because a change has been made, if the change is not reasonably expected to result in new or additional exposures to Cr(VI). For example, monitoring may be conducted in an establishment when welding was performed on steel with 15% chromium content. If the establishment switches to a steel with 10% chromium content without changing any other aspect of the work operation, then additional exposures to Cr(VI) would not reasonably be expected, and additional monitoring would not be required.

PERFORMANCE-ORIENTED OPTION

The performance-oriented option allows the employer to determine the 8-hour TWA exposure for each employee on the basis of any combination of air monitoring data (i.e., data obtained from initial and periodic Cr(VI) monitoring), historical monitoring data, or objective data sufficient to accurately characterize employee exposure to Cr(VI). This option is intended to allow employers flexibility in assessing the Cr(VI) exposures of their employees. Where the employer elects to follow this option, the exposure determination must be performed prior to the time the work operation commences and must provide the same degree of assurance that employee exposures have been correctly characterized as air monitoring would. The employer is expected to reevaluate employee exposures when there is any change in the production process, raw materials, equipment, personnel, work practices, or control methods that may result in new or additional exposures to Cr(VI).

EMPLOYEE NOTIFICATION

Employers must notify each affected employee if the exposure determination indicates that their exposure to Cr(VI) exceeds the PEL. "Affected employees" are all employees considered to be exposed above the PEL, including those employees who are not actually subject to personal monitoring, but who are represented by an employee who is sampled. Affected employees also include employees whose exposures have been deemed to be above the PEL on the basis of historical or objective data. The employer must either notify each affected employee in writing or post the determination results in an appropriate location accessible to all affected employees (e.g., a bulletin board accessible to all employees). In addition, the written notification must describe the corrective action(s) being taken by the employer to reduce the employee's exposure to or below the PEL (e.g., use of respirators or the engineering controls that will be implemented).

The general industry standard requires employers to notify employees within 15 working days from when monitoring results are received (or when the exposure determination is made for those following the performance-oriented option). In construction and shipyards, employers must notify each affected employee as soon as possible but not more than 5 working days later. A shorter time period for notification is mandated in construction and shipyards because of the often short duration of operations and employment in particular locations in these sectors.

ACCURACY OF MEASUREMENTS

The standard does not specify a particular method of sampling and analysis that must be used to measure employee exposures to Cr(VI). The employer may use any method as long as it meets certain accuracy requirements. Many laboratories presently have methods to measure Cr(VI) at the action level with at least the required degree of accuracy. One example of an acceptable method of monitoring and analysis is OSHA method ID215, which is a fully validated analytical method used by OSHA to measure Cr(VI) exposures.

OBSERVATION OF MONITORING

Employers must provide affected employees or their designated representatives an opportunity to observe any monitoring of employee exposure to Cr(VI) required by this standard. When observation of monitoring requires entry into an area where the use of protective clothing or equipment is required, the employer must provide the observer with these items, and assure that the observer uses them and complies with all other safety and health procedures.

OSHA
Occupational Safety and
Health Administration

Regulated Areas

The Cr(VI) standard for general industry includes requirements for regulated areas. The purpose of a regulated area is to ensure that employees are aware of the presence of Cr(VI) at levels above the PEL, and to limit Cr(VI) exposure to as few employees as possible by requiring the employer to mark areas where employee exposure is likely to exceed the PEL and limit access to these areas to authorized persons. The standard includes provisions for establishment of regulated areas; demarcation of regulated areas; and access to regulated areas. The requirements are not included in the standards for construction or shipyards because they are considered generally impracticable in these environments.

ESTABLISHMENT

Employers must establish regulated areas wherever an employee's exposure to Cr(VI) is, or can reasonably be expected to be, in excess of the PEL. Information obtained during the exposure determination can be used along with reasonable judgment to determine where regulated areas are required, and to establish the boundaries of regulated areas.

DEMARCATION

Regulated areas must be distinguished from the rest of the workplace in a manner that adequately establishes and alerts employees of the boundaries of the regulated area. The standard does not specify how employers are to demarcate regulated areas. Warning signs, barricades, lines and textured flooring, or other methods may be appropriate. Whatever methods are chosen must effectively warn employees not to enter the area unless they are authorized, and then only if they are using proper protective equipment, such as respirators.

ACCESS

Employers must limit access to regulated areas. The only individuals allowed access to a regulated area are:

- Persons authorized by the employer and required by work duties to be present in the regulated area (this may include maintenance and repair personnel, management, quality control engineers, or other personnel if job duties require their presence in the regulated area);
- Any person entering the area as a designated representative of employees to observe Cr(VI) exposure monitoring; or
- Any person authorized by the *Occupational Safety and Health Act* or regulations issued under it to be in a regulated area (e.g., OSHA enforcement personnel).

Methods of Compliance

Employers must use engineering and work practice controls as the primary means to reduce and maintain employee exposures to Cr(VI) to or below the PEL, unless the employer can demonstrate that such control measures are not feasible. Engineering controls include:

- Substitution (e.g., using a less toxic material instead of Cr(VI), or substituting a process that results in lower exposures for another type of process that results in higher exposures);

- Isolation (e.g., enclosing the source of exposure, or placing a barrier between employees and the source of exposure); and
- Ventilation (e.g., local exhaust systems that capture airborne Cr(VI) near its source and remove it from the workplace, or general ventilation that dilutes Cr(VI) concentrations by circulating large quantities of air – a local exhaust system is generally preferred to dilution ventilation because it provides a cleaner and healthier work environment).

Work practice controls involve adjustments in the way a task is performed. In many cases, work practice controls complement engineering controls in providing employee protection. For example, periodic inspection and maintenance of control equipment such as ventilation systems is an important work practice control. Frequently, equipment which is in disrepair will not perform normally. If equipment is routinely inspected, maintained, and repaired or replaced before failure is likely, there is less chance that hazardous exposures will occur.

Employees must know the way to perform their job tasks in order to minimize their exposure to Cr(VI) and to maximize the effectiveness of control measures. For example, if an exhaust hood is designed to provide local ventilation and an employee performs a task that generates Cr(VI) aerosols away from the exhaust hood, the control measure will be of no use. Good supervision further ensures that proper work practices are carried out by employees.

Employees' exposures can also be controlled by scheduling operations with the highest exposures at a time when the fewest employees are present. For example, routine cleanup operations that involve Cr(VI) releases might be performed at night or at times when the usual production staff is not present.

If feasible engineering and work practice controls are not sufficient to reduce employee exposure to or below the PEL, the employer must use them to reduce the exposure to the lowest level achievable. Respirators must then be used to reduce employee exposure to or below the PEL. The standards require primary reliance on engineering and work practice controls because they are generally reliable, provide consistent protection to a large number of employees, can be monitored, and can efficiently remove Cr(VI) from the workplace. Although an important method of protecting employees, effective use of respirators is more difficult to achieve. Use of respirators in the workplace also presents other safety and health concerns due to the physiological burdens on employees using respirators, and limitations on auditory, visual, and odor sensations.

There are two exceptions to the general requirement for primary use of engineering and work practice controls to reduce employee exposure to within permissible limits. The first exception applies to the painting of aircraft or large aircraft parts (e.g., the interior or exterior of whole aircraft, aircraft wings or tail sections, or comparably sized aircraft parts) in the aerospace industry. When such painting is performed, the employer must use engineering and work practice controls to reduce employee Cr(VI) exposures to or below 25 μg/m³ unless the employer can demonstrate that such controls are not feasible. Use of respirators is then required to limit exposures to or below the PEL.

The second exception to the general requirement for primary reliance on engineering and work practice controls applies where employers do not have employee exposures above the PEL for 30 or more days per year (12 consecutive months) from a particular process or task. Thus, if a particular process or task results in employee exposures to Cr(VI) that exceed the PEL on 29 or fewer days during any 12 consecutive months, the employer is allowed to use any combination of controls, including respirators alone, to achieve the PEL. The burden of proof is on the employer to demonstrate that a process or task will not cause employee exposures to remain above the PEL for 30 or more days per year. Historical data, objective data, or exposure monitoring data may be used for this purpose. Other information, such as production orders showing that processes involving Cr(VI) exposures are conducted on fewer than 30 days per year, may also be used.

Employers are not permitted to rotate employees to different jobs as a means of achieving compliance with the PEL. However, there is no general prohibition on employee rotation. Employers may rotate employees for other reasons, such as to provide cross-training on different tasks or to allow employees to alternate physically demanding tasks with less strenuous activities.

OSHA
**Occupational Safety and
Health Administration**

Respiratory Protection

When engineering and work practice controls cannot reduce employee exposure to Cr(VI) to within the PEL, employers must provide employees with respirators. Specifically, respirators are required during:

- Periods necessary to install or implement feasible engineering and work practice controls;
- Work operations, such as maintenance and repair activities, for which engineering and work practice controls are not feasible;
- Work operations for which an employer has implemented all feasible engineering and work practice controls and such controls are not sufficient to reduce exposures to or below the PEL;
- Work operations where employees are exposed above the PEL for fewer than 30 days per year, and the employer has elected not to implement engineering and work practice controls to achieve the PEL; or

- Emergencies (i.e., uncontrolled releases of Cr(VI) that result in significant and unexpected exposures; see definition of "Emergency" at pg. 5).

Where respirator use is required, the employer must establish a respiratory protection program in accordance with OSHA's Respiratory Protection standard (29 CFR 1910.134). The respiratory protection program addresses procedures for properly selecting and using respirators in the workplace. OSHA has prepared a separate Small Entity Compliance Guide for the Respiratory Protection standard (available at http://www.osha.gov/pls/publications/pubindex.list# 118) which provides additional information on the requirements of that standard.

Protective Work Clothing and Equipment

Employers must provide appropriate protective clothing and equipment wherever skin or eye contact with Cr(VI) is likely to present a hazard to employees. The employer is also required to ensure that employees use the clothing and equipment provided, and follow a number of specified practices to ensure that protective clothing and equipment is used and handled in a manner that is protective of employee health.

Protective work clothing and equipment is only that clothing and equipment that serves to protect employees from Cr(VI) hazards. Other clothing, work uniforms, tools or other apparatus that do not serve to protect employees from Cr(VI) hazards are not considered protective clothing and equipment under the standards.

PROVISION AND USE

In order to provide appropriate protective work clothing and equipment, the employer should assess the workplace to identify areas where a hazard is present or is likely to be present from skin or eye contact with Cr(VI). The employer should exercise common sense and use appropriate expertise in assessing hazards. A walk-through survey of the workplace is recommended to identify sources of employee Cr(VI) exposure. A

review of workplace injury and illness records is also recommended. Information obtained during this process provides a basis for evaluating potential hazards. Exposures must be evaluated on a case-by-case basis, taking into account factors such as the acidity or alkalinity of the Cr(VI)-containing compound or mixture as well as the magnitude and duration of exposure.

Where a hazard is identified, the employer must select the clothing and equipment needed to protect employees from Cr(VI) hazards. The type of protective clothing and equipment needed to protect employees from Cr(VI) hazards will depend on the potential for exposure and the conditions of use in the workplace. Examples of protective clothing and equipment that may be necessary include, but are not limited to, gloves, aprons, coveralls, foot coverings, and goggles.

The employer must exercise reasonable judgment in selecting the appropriate clothing and equipment to use to protect employees from hazards associated with Cr(VI) exposures. In some instances gloves may be all that is necessary to effectively protect an employee from hazardous Cr(VI) exposure. In other situations, such as when an employee is performing abrasive blasting on a structure covered with Cr(VI)-

containing paint, more extensive measures such as coveralls, head coverings, and goggles may be needed. The chemical and physical properties of the compound or mixture may also influence the choice of clothing and equipment to use. For example, a chrome plater may require an apron, gloves, and goggles to protect against possible splashes of chromic acid that could result in both Cr(VI) exposure and chemical burns. Other factors such as the size, flexibility, and cut and tear resistance of clothing and equipment should be considered in the selection process as well.

OSHA has issued a booklet, *Personal Protective Equipment* (OSHA Publication 3151, available at http://www. osha.gov/Publications/osha3151.pdf), that provides more information on assessment of workplace hazards and selection of appropriate protective clothing and equipment, as well as other factors related to the use of these items.

Employers must provide the clothing and equipment at no cost to the employee. Where protective clothing and equipment is required, the employer must ensure that it is used in the workplace.

REMOVAL AND STORAGE

The employer must ensure that employees remove protective clothing and equipment that has become contaminated with Cr(VI) at the end of their work shift or when they complete their tasks involving Cr(VI) exposure, whichever comes first. For example, if employees perform work tasks involving Cr(VI) exposure for the first two hours of a shift, and then perform tasks that do not involve Cr(VI) exposure for the remainder of the shift, they must remove their protective clothing after the exposure period (in this case, after the first two hours of the shift). If, however, employees are performing tasks involving Cr(VI) exposure intermittently throughout the day, or if employees are exposed to other contaminants where protective clothing and equipment are needed, they may wear the clothing and equipment until the completion of their shift. This requirement is intended to limit the duration of employees' exposure, and to prevent contamination from Cr(VI) residues on protective clothing reaching areas of the workplace where exposures would not otherwise occur.

The employer must not allow any employee to remove contaminated protective clothing or equipment from the workplace, except for those employees whose job it is to launder, clean, maintain, or dispose of the clothing or equipment. This requirement is intended to ensure that clothing contaminated with Cr(VI) is not carried to employees' cars and homes, which would increase the employee's exposure as well as exposing other individuals to Cr(VI) hazards.

When contaminated protective clothing or equipment is removed for laundering, cleaning, maintenance, or disposal, it must be stored and transported in sealed, impermeable bags or other closed, impermeable containers. Bags or containers of contaminated protective clothing or equipment that are removed for laundering, cleaning, maintenance, or disposal must be labeled in accordance with the requirements of OSHA's Hazard Communication standard (29 CFR 1910.1200). In general, the Hazard Communication standard requires that each container of hazardous chemicals leaving the workplace include a label that indicates the identity of the hazardous chemicals in the container, appropriate hazard warnings, and the name and address of a responsible party who can provide additional information on the hazardous chemicals. Use of impermeable containers and proper labeling practices serve to minimize contamination of the workplace and ensure that employees who later handle these items are protected.

CLEANING AND REPLACEMENT

The employer must clean, launder, repair and replace protective clothing and equipment as necessary to ensure that the effectiveness of the clothing and equipment is maintained. This requirement is intended to ensure that clothing and equipment continues to serve its intended purpose of protecting employees. The standards do not specify how often clothing and equipment must be cleaned, repaired, or replaced. The appropriate time intervals may vary widely based on the types of clothing and equipment used, Cr(VI) exposures, and other circumstances in the workplace. The obligation of the employer is to keep the clothing and equipment in the condition necessary to perform its protective functions.

Removal of Cr(VI) from protective clothing and equipment by blowing, shaking, or any other means that disperses Cr(VI) into the air or onto an employee's body is prohibited. Such actions would result in increased risk to employees from unnecessary exposure to airborne Cr(VI) as well as possible skin contact.

The employer must inform any person who launders or cleans protective clothing or equipment con-

taminated with Cr(VI) of the potentially harmful effects of Cr(VI) exposure, and that the clothing and equipment should be laundered or cleaned in a manner that minimizes skin or eye contact with Cr(VI) and prevents exposure to Cr(VI) in excess of the PEL. This requirement is intended to ensure that employees who clean or launder Cr(VI)-contaminated items are aware of the associated hazards so that they can take appropriate protective measures. The hazard warnings required on labels for containers of Cr(VI)-contaminated clothing and equipment, required by OSHA's Hazard Communication standard, are sufficient to indicate the potentially harmful effects of Cr(VI). An additional statement (i.e., a statement indi-

cating that the clothing and equipment should be handled in a manner that minimizes skin or eye contact with Cr(VI) and effectively prevents exposure to Cr(VI) in excess of the PEL) could be added to the label to fulfill this requirement. The employer is not expected to specify particular work practices that must be followed to achieve these objectives.

The employer is responsible for ensuring that protective work clothes and equipment are cleaned and properly disposed of. The employer should also conduct inspections and, when necessary, repair or replace protective work clothing and equipment to ensure its effectiveness.

Hygiene Areas and Practices

Employers must provide adequate hygiene facilities and ensure that employees comply with basic hygiene practices that serve to minimize exposure to Cr(VI). The standards include requirements for change rooms and washing facilities, ensuring that Cr(VI) exposure in eating and drinking areas is minimized, and a prohibition on certain practices that may contribute to Cr(VI) exposure.

CHANGE ROOMS

Where employees must change out of their street clothes to use protective clothing and equipment required by the standard, change rooms must be provided. The change rooms must be equipped with separate storage facilities (e.g., lockers) for protective clothing and equipment and for street clothes, and these facilities must prevent contamination of street clothes. Preventing contamination of street clothing limits exposures that would otherwise occur after the work shift ends, and avoids potential contamination of employees' cars and homes. Change rooms also provide privacy to employees while they change their clothes.

Change rooms are only required where removal of street clothes is necessary. For example, in a workplace where gloves are the only protective clothing used, change rooms are not necessary. Similarly, if disposable protective clothing can be effectively worn over street clothes, change rooms would not be required.

WASHING FACILITIES

Readily accessible washing facilities capable of removing Cr(VI) from the skin must be provided where skin contact with Cr(VI) occurs. Washing facilities must conform with OSHA's existing sanitation requirements (29 CFR 1910.141 for general industry; 29 CFR 1926.51 for construction). The employer must ensure that affected employees use these facilities when necessary. Also, the employer must ensure that employees who have skin contact with Cr(VI) wash their hands and faces at the end of the work shift and prior to eating, drinking, smoking, chewing tobacco or gum, applying cosmetics, or using the toilet. Washing diminishes the period of time that Cr(VI) is in contact with the skin, removes any residual Cr(VI) contamination, and protects against further exposure.

EATING AND DRINKING AREAS

Whenever an employer allows employees to consume food or beverages at a worksite where Cr(VI) is present, the employer must ensure that eating and drinking areas and surfaces are maintained as free as practicable of Cr(VI). Employers are also required to ensure that employees do not enter eating and drinking areas wearing Cr(VI)-contaminated protective clothing or equipment, unless the protective clothing or equipment is properly cleaned beforehand. The employer may use any method to remove surface Cr(VI) from clothing and equipment, as long as that method does not disperse Cr(VI) into the air or onto an employee's body. For example, a HEPA-filtered vacuum may be used to remove Cr(VI) contamination from an employee's clothing prior to entering the eating and drinking area.

PROHIBITED ACTIVITIES

The standards prohibit certain activities that are likely to result in unnecessary Cr(VI) exposures. The employer must ensure that employees do not eat, drink, smoke, chew tobacco or gum, or apply cosmetics in regulated areas, or in areas where skin or eye contact with Cr(VI) occurs. Products associated with these activities, such as food or cigarettes, must not be carried into or stored in regulated areas or areas where skin or eye contact with Cr(VI) occurs.

Housekeeping

The Cr(VI) standard for general industry includes requirements for housekeeping measures. Proper housekeeping measures are important, where practicable, because they minimize additional sources of exposure to Cr(VI) that engineering controls are generally not designed to address. The standard includes provisions addressing general housekeeping requirements; cleaning methods; and disposal of materials contaminated with Cr(VI). These requirements are not included in the standards for construction or shipyards because they are considered generally impracticable in these environments.

GENERAL REQUIREMENTS

Employers must ensure that:
- All surfaces are maintained as free as practicable of accumulations of Cr(VI); and
- All spills and releases of Cr(VI)-containing material are cleaned up promptly.

Cr(VI) deposited on ledges, equipment, floors, and other surfaces should be removed as soon as practicable to prevent it from becoming airborne and to minimize the likelihood that skin contact will occur. Spills should be rapidly contained and cleaned up without delay.

CLEANING METHODS

Surfaces contaminated with Cr(VI) must be cleaned by HEPA-filtered vacuuming or other methods that minimize exposure to Cr(VI). Other acceptable cleaning methods include wet methods, such as wet sweeping or wet scrubbing. Dry methods (e.g., dry shoveling, dry sweeping, and dry brushing) are generally prohibited because of the potential for dispersal of Cr(VI) into the air. Employers are only allowed to use dry methods in cases where HEPA-filtered vacuuming or other methods that minimize the likelihood of exposure to Cr(VI) have been tried and found not to be effective.

Use of compressed air for cleaning surfaces is also generally inappropriate because of the potential for dispersal of Cr(VI) into the air. Compressed air must not be used for cleaning surfaces unless it is used in conjunction with a ventilation system designed to capture the dust cloud, or if no alternative method is feasible.

Cleaning equipment must be handled in a manner that minimizes the reentry of Cr(VI) into the workplace. HEPA-filtered vacuum equipment must be cleaned and maintained carefully to avoid unnecessary exposures to Cr(VI). Filters must be changed when needed, and the contents of the bags must be disposed of properly to avoid unnecessary Cr(VI) exposures.

DISPOSAL OF CONTAMINATED MATERIALS

Waste, scrap, debris, and any other materials contaminated with Cr(VI) that are consigned for disposal must be disposed of in sealed, impermeable bags or other closed, impermeable containers. For example, the employer may wrap a pallet in plastic to create an impermeable barrier between employees and the Cr(VI) contaminated waste, scrap or debris. Another example would be to use a sealed barrel. Bags or containers of waste, scrap, debris, and any other materials contaminated with Cr(VI) that are consigned for disposal must be labeled in accordance with the requirements of OSHA's Hazard Communication standard (29 CFR 1910.1200).

OSHA
Occupational Safety and
Health Administration

Medical Surveillance

The intent of medical surveillance is to determine, where reasonably possible, if an individual can be exposed to the Cr(VI) present in his or her workplace without experiencing adverse health effects; to identify Cr(VI)-related adverse health effects when they do occur so that appropriate intervention measures can be taken; and to determine an employee's fitness to use personal protective equipment such as respirators. The standards specify which employees must be offered medical surveillance; when medical examinations must be offered; the contents of the examination; information that the employer must provide to the physician or other licensed health care professional (PLHCP) who performs the examination; and the contents of the written medical opinion that the employer must obtain from the PLHCP.

All medical examinations and procedures required by the standards must be performed by or under the supervision of a PLHCP. Medical surveillance must be provided at no cost to employees, and at a reasonable time and place. If participation requires travel away from the worksite, the employer must bear the cost. Employees must be paid for time spent taking medical examinations, including travel time.

EMPLOYEES PROVIDED MEDICAL SURVEILLANCE

Medical surveillance must be provided to employees who are:

- Exposed to Cr(VI) at or above the action level (2.5 µg/m³ Cr(VI) as an 8-hour time-weighted average) for 30 or more days a year;
- Experiencing signs or symptoms of the adverse health effects associated with Cr(VI) exposure (e.g., blistering lesions, redness or itchiness of exposed skin, shortness of breath or wheezing that worsens at work, nosebleeds, a whistling sound while inhaling or exhaling); or
- Exposed in an emergency (i.e., an uncontrolled release of Cr(VI) that results in significant and unexpected exposures; see definition of "Emergency" at pg. 5).

FREQUENCY OF MEDICAL EXAMINATIONS

Medical examinations must be provided:

- Within 30 days after initial assignment to a job involving Cr(VI) exposure, unless the employee has received an examination that meets the requirements of the standard within the last 12 months;

- Annually;
- Within 30 days after a PLHCP's written medical opinion recommends an additional examination;
- Whenever an employee shows signs or symptoms of the adverse health effects associated with Cr(VI) exposure;
- Within 30 days after exposure during an emergency which results in an uncontrolled release of Cr(VI); or
- At the termination of employment, unless the last examination provided was less than six months prior to the date of termination.

CONTENTS OF THE EXAMINATION

A medical examination provided under the standard consists of:

- A medical and work history which focuses on: the employee's past, present, and anticipated future exposure to Cr(VI); any history of respiratory system dysfunction; any history of asthma, dermatitis, skin ulceration, or nasal septum perforation; and smoking status and history;
- A physical examination of the skin and respiratory tract; and
- Any additional tests that the examining PLHCP considers to be appropriate for that individual.

The standards do not specify specific tests or procedures that must be provided to all employees. Rather, the information obtained from the medical and work history along with the physical examination of the skin and respiratory tract (the main targets of Cr(VI) toxicity) allow the PLHCPs to use their medical expertise to determine what tests, if any, are warranted.

INFORMATION PROVIDED TO THE PLHCP

The employer must ensure that the PLHCP has a copy of the Cr(VI) standard, and must provide the PLHCP with:

- A description of the affected employee's former, current, and anticipated duties as they relate to Cr(VI) exposure;
- Information on the employee's former, current, and anticipated Cr(VI) exposure levels;
- A description of any personal protective equipment used or to be used by the employee, including when and for how long the employee has used that equipment; and

- Information from records of employment-related medical examinations previously provided to the affected employee.

THE WRITTEN MEDICAL OPINION

The employer must obtain a written medical opinion from the PLHCP for each medical examination performed. The written medical opinion must be obtained within 30 days of the examination, and must contain:

- The PLHCP's opinion as to whether the employee has any detected medical condition(s) that would place the employee at increased risk of material impairment to health from further exposure to Cr(VI);

- Any recommended limitations on the employee's exposure to Cr(VI) or on the use of personal protective equipment such as respirators; and
- A statement that the PLHCP has explained to the employee the results of the medical examination, including any medical conditions related to Cr(VI) exposure that require further evaluation or treatment, and any special provisions for use of protective clothing or equipment.

The PLHCP must not reveal to the employer any specific findings or diagnoses that are not related to workplace Cr(VI) exposure. The employer is required to provide a copy of the written medical opinion to the examined employee within two weeks after receiving it.

Communication of Cr(VI) Hazards to Employees

To protect against illnesses and injuries from Cr(VI) exposures, it is critically important that employees recognize the hazards associated with exposure to Cr(VI) and understand the measures they can take to protect themselves. OSHA's Hazard Communication standard (29 CFR 1910.1200) establishes requirements for employers to provide employees with information on hazardous chemicals such as Cr(VI) through comprehensive chemical hazard communication programs that include material safety data sheets (MSDSs), labels, and employee training. Employers must follow the requirements of the Hazard Communication standard with regard to employees exposed to Cr(VI). These requirements include informing employees of any operations in their work area where Cr(VI) is present and training employees on:

- The methods that may be used to detect Cr(VI) in the work area:
- The hazards of Cr(VI); and
- Measures employees can take to protect themselves from these hazards (e.g., appropriate work practices, emergency procedures, and protective equipment to be used).

In addition, the Cr(VI) standards require the employer to provide information and training sufficient to ensure that employees exposed to Cr(VI) can demonstrate knowledge of:

- The requirements of the Cr(VI) standard; and
- The medical surveillance program required by the standard, including recognition of the signs and symptoms of adverse health effects that may result from Cr(VI) exposure.

The employer must also make a copy of the Cr(VI) standard available without cost to all affected employees.

The standards do not specify how training is to be provided. Classroom instruction, video presentations, informal discussions, written materials, or other methods may be appropriate. The employer may select whatever methods are most effective in a specific workplace. Similarly, the standards do not require employers to provide additional training at periodic intervals. Training must be provided as often as is necessary to ensure that employees are aware of the Cr(VI) hazards in their workplace and understand the protective measures available to them.

OSHA
Occupational Safety and
Health Administration

Recordkeeping

Accurate records can demonstrate employer compliance with the standard, and can assist in diagnosing and identifying workplace-related illnesses. Therefore, employers are required to maintain records of employee Cr(VI) exposures (including air monitoring data, historical monitoring data, and objective data) as well as records of medical surveillance provided under the standard.

AIR MONITORING DATA

Employers must keep an accurate record of all air monitoring performed to comply with the standard. The record must indicate:

- The date of the measurement for each sample taken;
- The operation involving exposure to Cr(VI) that was monitored;
- Sampling and analytical methods used and evidence of their accuracy;
- The number, duration, and results of samples taken;
- The type of personal protective equipment used (e.g., type of respirators worn); and
- The name, social security number, and job classification of all employees represented by the monitoring, specifying which employees were actually monitored.

HISTORICAL MONITORING DATA

When an employer relies on historical monitoring data to determine employee exposures to Cr(VI), an accurate record of the historical monitoring data must be maintained. The record must show:

- That the data were collected using methods that meet the accuracy requirements of the standard (i.e., the method of monitoring and analysis used must measure Cr(VI) to within an accuracy of ± 25% and to within a statistical confidence level of 95%);
- That the processes and work practices, the characteristics of the Cr(VI)-containing material being handled, and the environmental conditions at the time the data were obtained are the same as those on the job for which exposure is being determined; and

- Any other data relevant to the operations, materials, processing, and employee exposures.

OBJECTIVE DATA

When an employer relies on objective data to comply with the Cr(VI) standard, an accurate record of the objective data must be maintained. The record must indicate:

- The chromium-containing material in question;
- The source of the objective data;
- The testing protocol and results of testing, or analysis of the material for the release of Cr(VI);
- A description of the process, operation, or activity and how the data support the determination; and
- Any other data relevant to the process, operation, activity, material, or employee exposures.

MEDICAL SURVEILLANCE

The employer must maintain an accurate record for each employee provided medical surveillance under the standard. The record must include the following information about the employee:

- Name and social security number;
- A copy of the PLHCP's written opinions; and
- A copy of the information that the employer was required to provide to the PLHCP (i.e., a description of the employee's duties as they relate to occupational Cr(VI) exposure; the employee's Cr(VI) exposure levels; a description of the personal protective equipment used by the employee; and information from previous employment-related medical examinations).

Exposure and medical records must be maintained and made available to employees and their representatives. A separate OSHA standard (29 CFR 1910.1020, Access to Employee Exposure and Medical Records) addresses requirements for maintaining these records. In general, exposure records must be kept for at least 30 years, and medical records must be kept for the duration of employment plus 30 years. It is necessary to keep these records for extended periods because cancer often cannot be detected until 20 or more years after exposure, and exposure and medical records can assist in diagnosing and identifying the cause of disease.

Dates

Employers with 20 or more employees must comply with the requirements of the standards (except the requirements for use of engineering controls) by November 27, 2006. Employers with 19 or fewer employees must comply with the requirements of the standards (except the requirements for use of engineering controls) by May 30, 2007. During the time prior to these compliance dates, employers should take steps to ensure that they are able to meet the requirements of the standards by the start-up dates. Initial exposure assessments should be completed, respiratory protection programs should be established where necessary, appropriate respirators should be obtained, regulated areas should be established where required, appropriate protective work clothing

and equipment should be acquired, arrangements should be made for provision of medical surveillance, and other measures necessary to comply with the provisions of the standards should be taken. All requirements of the standards (except those for engineering controls) will be enforced as of the specified dates.

Engineering controls required by the standards must be in place by May 31, 2010. This date applies to all employers, regardless of size. This additional time for implementation of engineering controls is allotted to allow sufficient time for the process of designing, obtaining, and installing equipment and adopting new work methods.

OSHA can provide extensive help through a variety of programs, including technical assistance about effective safety and health programs, state plans, workplace consultations, voluntary protection programs, strategic partnerships, training and education, and more. An overall commitment to workplace safety and health can add value to your business, to your workplace and to your life.

SAFETY AND HEALTH PROGRAM MANAGEMENT GUIDELINES

Effective management of employee safety and health protection is a decisive factor in reducing the extent and severity of work-related injuries and illnesses and their related costs. In fact, an effective safety and health program forms the basis of good employee protection and can save time and money (about $4 for every dollar spent) and increase productivity and reduce employee injuries, illnesses and related workers' compensation costs.

To assist employers and employees in developing effective safety and health programs, OSHA published recommended *Safety and Health Program Management Guidelines* (54 *Federal Register* (16): 3904-3916, January 26, 1989). These voluntary guidelines apply to all places of employment covered by OSHA.

The guidelines identify four general elements critical to the development of a successful safety and health management program:

- Management leadership and employee involvement.
- Work analysis.
- Hazard prevention and control.
- Safety and health training.

The guidelines recommend specific actions, under each of these general elements, to achieve an effective safety and health program. The *Federal Register* notice is available online at www.osha.gov

STATE PROGRAMS

The Occupational Safety and Health Act of 1970 (*OSH Act*) encourages states to develop and operate their own job safety and health plans. OSHA approves and monitors these plans. Twenty-four states, Puerto Rico and the Virgin Islands currently operate approved state plans: 22 cover both private and public (state and local government) employment; the Connecticut, New Jersey, New York and Virgin Islands plans cover the public sector only. States and territories with their own OSHA-approved occupational safety and health plans must adopt standards identical to, or at least as effective as, the Federal standards.

CONSULTATION SERVICES

Consultation assistance is available on request to employers who want help in establishing and maintaining a safe and healthful workplace. Largely funded by OSHA, the service is provided at no cost to the employer. Primarily developed for smaller employers with more hazardous operations, the consultation service is delivered by state governments employing professional safety and health consultants. Comprehensive assistance includes an appraisal of all mechanical systems, work practices and occupational safety and health hazards of the workplace and all aspects of the employer's present job safety and health program. In addition, the service offers assistance to employers in developing and implementing an effective safety and health program. No penalties are proposed or citations issued for hazards identified by the consultant. OSHA provides consultation assistance to the employer with the assurance that his or her name and firm and any information about the workplace will not be routinely reported to OSHA enforcement staff.

Under the consultation program, certain exemplary employers may request participation in OSHA's Safety and Health Achievement Recognition Program (SHARP). Eligibility for participation in SHARP includes receiving a comprehensive consultation visit, demonstrating exemplary achievements in workplace safety and health by abating all identified hazards and developing an excellent safety and health program.

Employers accepted into SHARP may receive an exemption from programmed inspections (not complaint or accident investigation inspections) for a period of one year. For more information concerning consultation assistance, see the OSHA website at www.osha.gov

VOLUNTARY PROTECTION PROGRAMS (VPP)

Voluntary Protection Programs and on-site consultation services, when coupled with an effective enforcement program, expand employee protection to help meet the goals of the *OSH Act*. The three levels of VPP are Star, Merit, and Demonstration designed to recognize outstanding achievements by companies that have successfully incorporated comprehensive safety and health programs into their total management system. The VPPs motivate others to achieve excellent safety and health results in the same outstanding way as they establish a cooperative relationship between employers, employees and OSHA.

For additional information on VPP and how to apply, contact the OSHA regional offices listed in Appendix III. B.

STRATEGIC PARTNERSHIP PROGRAM

OSHA's Strategic Partnership Program, the newest member of OSHA's cooperative programs, helps encourage, assist and recognize the efforts of partners to eliminate serious workplace hazards and achieve a high level of employee safety and health. Whereas OSHA's Consultation Program and VPP entail one-on-one relationships between OSHA and individual worksites, most strategic partnerships seek to have a broader impact by building cooperative relationships with groups of employers and employees. These partnerships are voluntary, cooperative relationships between OSHA, employers, employee representatives and others (e.g., trade unions, trade and professional associations, universities and other government agencies).

For more information on this and other cooperative programs, contact your nearest OSHA office, or visit OSHA's website at www.osha.gov

ALLIANCE PROGRAMS

The Alliance Program enables organizations committed to workplace safety and health to collaborate with OSHA to prevent injuries and illnesses in the workplace. OSHA and the Alliance participants work together to reach out to, educate and lead the nation's employers and their employees in improving and advancing workplace safety and health.

Groups that can form an Alliance with OSHA include employers, labor unions, trade or professional groups, educational institutions and government agencies. In some cases, organizations may be building on existing relationships with OSHA that were developed through other cooperative programs.

There are few formal program requirements for Alliances and the agreements do not include an enforcement component. However, OSHA and the participating organizations must define, implement and meet a set of short- and long-term goals that fall into three categories: training and education; outreach and communication; and promoting the national dialogue on workplace safety and health.

OSHA TRAINING AND EDUCATION

OSHA area offices offer a variety of information services, such as compliance assistance, technical advice, publications, audiovisual aids and speakers for special engagements. OSHA's Training Institute in Arlington Heights, IL, provides basic and advanced courses in safety and health for Federal and state compliance officers, state consultants, Federal agency personnel, and private sector employers, employees and their representatives.

The OSHA Training Institute also has established OSHA Training Institute Education Centers to address the increased demand for its courses from the private sector and from other Federal agencies. These centers are nonprofit colleges, universities and other organizations that have been selected after a competition for participation in the program.

OSHA also provides funds to nonprofit organizations, through grants, to conduct workplace training and education in subjects where OSHA believes there is a lack of workplace training. Grants are awarded annually. Grant recipients are expected to contribute 20 percent of the total grant cost.

For more information on grants, training and education, contact the OSHA Training Institute, Office of Training and Education, 2020 South Arlington Heights Road, Arlington Heights, IL 60005, (847) 297-4810 or see "Outreach" on OSHA's website at www.osha.gov. For further information on any OSHA program, contact your nearest OSHA area or regional office listed at the end of this publication.

INFORMATION AVAILABLE ELECTRONICALLY

OSHA has a variety of materials and tools available on its website at www.osha.gov. These include *e-Tools* such as *Expert Advisors, Electronic Compliance Assistance Tools (e-cats), Technical Links*; regulations, directives and publications; videos and other information for employers and employees. OSHA's software programs and compliance assistance tools walk you through challenging safety and health issues and common problems to find the best solutions for your workplace.

OSHA
Occupational Safety and
Health Administration

A wide variety of OSHA materials, including standards, interpretations, directives, and more, can be purchased on CD-ROM from the U.S. Government Printing Office, Superintendent of Documents, phone toll-free (866) 512-1800.

OSHA PUBLICATIONS

OSHA has an extensive publications program. For a listing of free or sales items, visit OSHA's website at www.osha.gov or contact the OSHA Publications Office, U.S. Department of Labor, 200 Constitution Avenue, NW, N-3101, Washington, DC 20210. Telephone (202) 693-1888 or fax to (202) 693-2498.

CONTACTING OSHA

To report an emergency, file a complaint or seek OSHA advice, assistance or products, call (800) 321-OSHA or contact your nearest OSHA regional or area office listed in Appendix III. The teletypewriter (TTY) number is (877) 889-5627.

You can also file a complaint online and obtain more information on OSHA Federal and state programs by visiting OSHA's website at www.osha.gov

GENERAL INDUSTRY STANDARD

§1910.1026 Chromium (VI)

(a) SCOPE.

(1) This standard applies to occupational exposures to chromium (VI) in all forms and compounds in general industry, except:

(2) Exposures that occur in the application of pesticides regulated by the Environmental Protection Agency or another Federal government agency (e.g., the treatment of wood with preservatives);

(3) Exposures to portland cement; or

(4) Where the employer has objective data demonstrating that a material containing chromium or a specific process, operation, or activity involving chromium cannot release dusts, fumes, or mists of chromium (VI) in concentrations at or above 0.5 µg/m³ as an 8-hour time-weighted average (TWA) under any expected conditions of use.

(b) DEFINITIONS.

For the purposes of this section the following definitions apply:

Action level means a concentration of airborne chromium (VI) of 2.5 micrograms per cubic meter of air (2.5 µg/m³) calculated as an 8-hour time-weighted average (TWA).

Assistant Secretary means the Assistant Secretary of Labor for Occupational Safety and Health, U.S. Department of Labor, or designee.

Chromium (VI) [hexavalent chromium or Cr(VI)] means chromium with a valence of positive six, in any form and in any compound.

Director means the Director of the National Institute for Occupational Safety and Health (NIOSH), U.S. Department of Health and Human Services, or designee.

Emergency means any occurrence that results, or is likely to result, in an uncontrolled release of chromium (VI). If an incidental release of chromium (VI) can be controlled at the time of release by employees in the immediate release area, or by maintenance personnel, it is not an emergency.

Employee exposure means the exposure to airborne chromium (VI) that would occur if the employee were not using a respirator.

High-efficiency particulate air [HEPA] filter means a filter that is at least 99.97 percent efficient in removing mono-dispersed particles of 0.3 micrometers in diameter or larger.

Historical monitoring data means data from chromium (VI) monitoring conducted prior to May 30, 2006, obtained during work operations conducted under workplace conditions closely resembling the processes, types of material, control methods, work practices, and environmental conditions in the employer's current operations.

Objective data means information such as air monitoring data from industry-wide surveys or calculations based on the composition or chemical and physical properties of a substance demonstrating the employee exposure to chromium (VI) associated with a particular product or material or a specific process, operation, or activity. The data must reflect workplace conditions closely resembling the processes, types of material, control methods, work practices, and environmental conditions in the employer's current operations.

Physician or other licensed health care professional [PLHCP] is an individual whose legally permitted scope of practice (i.e., license, registration, or certification) allows him or her to independently provide or be delegated the responsibility to provide some or all of the particular health care services required by paragraph (k) of this section.

Regulated area means an area, demarcated by the employer, where an employee's exposure to airborne concentrations of chromium (VI) exceeds, or can reasonably be expected to exceed, the PEL.

This section means this 1910.1026 chromium (VI) standard.

(c) PERMISSIBLE EXPOSURE LIMIT (PEL).

The employer shall ensure that no employee is exposed to an airborne concentration of chromium (VI) in excess of 5 micrograms per cubic meter of air (5 µg/m³), calculated as an 8-hour time-weighted average (TWA).

(d) EXPOSURE DETERMINATION.

(1) **General.** Each employer who has a workplace or work operation covered by this section shall determine the 8-hour TWA exposure for each employee

Occupational Safety and Health Administration

exposed to chromium (VI). This determination shall be made in accordance with either paragraph (d)(2) or paragraph (d)(3) of this section.

(2) Scheduled monitoring option.

(i) The employer shall perform initial monitoring to determine the 8-hour TWA exposure for each employee on the basis of a sufficient number of personal breathing zone air samples to accurately characterize full shift exposure on each shift, for each job classification, in each work area. Where an employer does representative sampling instead of sampling all employees in order to meet this requirement, the employer shall sample the employee(s) expected to have the highest chromium (VI) exposures.

(ii) If initial monitoring indicates that employee exposures are below the action level, the employer may discontinue monitoring for those employees whose exposures are represented by such monitoring.

(iii) If monitoring reveals employee exposures to be at or above the action level, the employer shall perform periodic monitoring at least every six months.

(iv) If monitoring reveals employee exposures to be above the PEL, the employer shall perform periodic monitoring at least every three months.

(v) If periodic monitoring indicates that employee exposures are below the action level, and the result is confirmed by the result of another monitoring taken at least seven days later, the employer may discontinue the monitoring for those employees whose exposures are represented by such monitoring.

(vi) The employer shall perform additional monitoring when there has been any change in the production process, raw materials, equipment, personnel, work practices, or control methods that may result in new or additional exposures to chromium (VI), or when the employer has any reason to believe that new or additional exposures have occurred.

(3) Performance-oriented option. The employer shall determine the 8-hour TWA exposure for each employee on the basis of any combination of air monitoring data, historical monitoring data, or objective data sufficient to accurately characterize employee exposure to chromium (VI).

(4) Employee notification of determination results.

(i) Where the exposure determination indicates that employee exposure exceeds the PEL, within 15 working days the employer shall either post the results in an appropriate location that is accessible to all affected employees or shall notify each affected employee individually in writing of the results.

(ii) Whenever the exposure determination indicates that employee exposure is above the PEL, the employer shall describe in the written notification the corrective action being taken to reduce employee exposure to or below the PEL.

(5) Accuracy of measurement. Where air monitoring is performed to comply with the requirements of this section, the employer shall use a method of monitoring and analysis that can measure chromium (VI) to within an accuracy of plus or minus 25 percent (+/-25%) and can produce accurate measurements to within a statistical confidence level of 95 percent for airborne concentrations at or above the action level.

(6) Observation of monitoring.

(i) Where air monitoring is performed to comply with the requirements of this section, the employer shall provide affected employees or their designated representatives an opportunity to observe any monitoring of employee exposure to chromium (VI).

(ii) When observation of monitoring requires entry into an area where the use of protective clothing or equipment is required, the employer shall provide the observer with clothing and equipment and shall assure that the observer uses such clothing and equipment and complies with all other applicable safety and health procedures.

(e) REGULATED AREAS.

(1) Establishment. The employer shall establish a regulated area wherever an employee's exposure to airborne concentrations of chromium (VI) is, or can reasonably be expected to be, in excess of the PEL.

(2) Demarcation. The employer shall ensure that regulated areas are demarcated from the rest of the workplace in a manner that adequately establishes and alerts employees of the boundaries of the regulated area.

(3) Access. The employer shall limit access to regulated areas to:

(i) Persons authorized by the employer and required by work duties to be present in the regulated area;

(ii) Any person entering such an area as a designated representative of employees for the purpose of exercising the right to observe monitoring procedures under paragraph (d) of this section; or

(iii) Any person authorized by the *Occupational Safety and Health Act* or regulations issued under it to be in a regulated area.

(1) Engineering and work practice controls.

(i) Except as permitted in paragraph (f)(1)(ii) and paragraph (f)(1)(iii) of this section, the employer shall use engineering and work practice controls to reduce and maintain employee exposure to chromium (VI) to or below the PEL unless the employer can demonstrate that such controls are not feasible. Wherever feasible engineering and work practice controls are not sufficient to reduce employee exposure to or below the PEL, the employer shall use them to reduce employee exposure to the lowest levels achievable, and shall supplement them by the use of respiratory protection that complies with the requirements of paragraph (g) of this section.

(ii) Where painting of aircraft or large aircraft parts is performed in the aerospace industry, the employer shall use engineering and work practice controls to reduce and maintain employee exposure to chromium (VI) to or below 25 $\mu g/m^3$ unless the employer can demonstrate that such controls are not feasible. The employer shall supplement such engineering and work practice controls with the use of respiratory protection that complies with the requirements of paragraph (g) of this section to achieve the PEL.

(iii) Where the employer can demonstrate that a process or task does not result in any employee exposure to chromium (VI) above the PEL for 30 or more days per year (12 consecutive months), the requirement to implement engineering and work practice controls to achieve the PEL does not apply to that process or task.

(2) Prohibition of rotation. The employer shall not rotate employees to different jobs to achieve compliance with the PEL.

(1) General. The employer shall provide respiratory protection for employees during:

(i) Periods necessary to install or implement feasible engineering and work practice controls;

(ii) Work operations, such as maintenance and repair activities, for which engineering and work practice controls are not feasible;

(iii) Work operations for which an employer has implemented all feasible engineering and work practice controls and such controls are not sufficient to reduce exposures to or below the PEL;

(iv) Work operations where employees are exposed above the PEL for fewer than 30 days per year,

and the employer has elected not to implement engineering and work practice controls to achieve the PEL; or

(v) Emergencies.

(2) Respiratory protection program. Where respirator use is required by this section, the employer shall institute a respiratory protection program in accordance with 29 CFR 1910.134.

(1) Provision and use. Where a hazard is present or is likely to be present from skin or eye contact with chromium (VI), the employer shall provide appropriate personal protective clothing and equipment at no cost to employees, and shall ensure that employees use such clothing and equipment.

(2) Removal and storage.

(i) The employer shall ensure that employees remove all protective clothing and equipment contaminated with chromium (VI) at the end of the work shift or at the completion of their tasks involving chromium (VI) exposure, whichever comes first.

(ii) The employer shall ensure that no employee removes chromium (VI)-contaminated protective clothing or equipment from the workplace, except for those employees whose job it is to launder, clean, maintain, or dispose of such clothing or equipment.

(iii) When contaminated protective clothing or equipment is removed for laundering, cleaning, maintenance, or disposal, the employer shall ensure that it is stored and transported in sealed, impermeable bags or other closed, impermeable containers.

(iv) Bags or containers of contaminated protective clothing or equipment that are removed from change rooms for laundering, cleaning, maintenance, or disposal shall be labeled in accordance with the requirements of the Hazard Communication standard, (29 CFR 1910.1200).

(3) Cleaning and replacement.

(i) The employer shall clean, launder, repair and replace all protective clothing and equipment required by this section as needed to maintain its effectiveness.

(ii) The employer shall prohibit the removal of chromium (VI) from protective clothing and equipment by blowing, shaking, or any other means that disperses chromium (VI) into the air or onto an employee's body.

(iii) The employer shall inform any person who launders or cleans protective clothing or equipment

contaminated with chromium (VI) of the potentially harmful effects of exposure to chromium (VI) and that the clothing and equipment should be laundered or cleaned in a manner that minimizes skin or eye contact with chromium (VI) and effectively prevents the release of airborne chromium (VI) in excess of the PEL.

(i) HYGIENE AREAS AND PRACTICES.

(1) General. Where protective clothing and equipment is required, the employer shall provide change rooms in conformance with 29 CFR 1910.141. Where skin contact with chromium (VI) occurs, the employer shall provide washing facilities in conformance with 29 CFR 1910.141. Eating and drinking areas provided by the employer shall also be in conformance with §1910.141.

(2) Change rooms. The employer shall assure that change rooms are equipped with separate storage facilities for protective clothing and equipment and for street clothes, and that these facilities prevent cross-contamination.

(3) Washing facilities.

(i) The employer shall provide readily accessible washing facilities capable of removing chromium (VI) from the skin, and shall ensure that affected employees use these facilities when necessary.

(ii) The employer shall ensure that employees who have skin contact with chromium (VI) wash their hands and faces at the end of the work shift and prior to eating, drinking, smoking, chewing tobacco or gum, applying cosmetics, or using the toilet.

(4) Eating and drinking areas.

(i) Whenever the employer allows employees to consume food or beverages at a worksite where chromium (VI) is present, the employer shall ensure that eating and drinking areas and surfaces are maintained as free as practicable of chromium (VI).

(ii) The employer shall ensure that employees do not enter eating and drinking areas with protective work clothing or equipment unless surface chromium (VI) has been removed from the clothing and equipment by methods that do not disperse chromium (VI) into the air or onto an employee's body.

(5) Prohibited activities. The employer shall ensure that employees do not eat, drink, smoke, chew tobacco or gum, or apply cosmetics in regulated areas, or in areas where skin or eye contact with chromium (VI) occurs; or carry the products associated with these activities, or store such products in these areas.

(j) HOUSEKEEPING.

(1) General. The employer shall ensure that:

(i) All surfaces are maintained as free as practicable of accumulations of chromium (VI).

(ii) All spills and releases of chromium (VI) containing material are cleaned up promptly.

(2) Cleaning methods.

(i) The employer shall ensure that surfaces contaminated with chromium (VI) are cleaned by HEPA-filter vacuuming or other methods that minimize the likelihood of exposure to chromium (VI).

(ii) Dry shoveling, dry sweeping, and dry brushing may be used only where HEPA-filtered vacuuming or other methods that minimize the likelihood of exposure to chromium (VI) have been tried and found not to be effective.

(iii) The employer shall not allow compressed air to be used to remove chromium (VI) from any surface unless:

(A) The compressed air is used in conjunction with a ventilation system designed to capture the dust cloud created by the compressed air; or

(B) No alternative method is feasible.

(iv) The employer shall ensure that cleaning equipment is handled in a manner that minimizes the reentry of chromium (VI) into the workplace.

(3) Disposal. The employer shall ensure that:

(i) Waste, scrap, debris, and any other materials contaminated with chromium (VI) and consigned for disposal are collected and disposed of in sealed, impermeable bags or other closed, impermeable containers.

(ii) Bags or containers of waste, scrap, debris, and any other materials contaminated with chromium (VI) that are consigned for disposal are labeled in accordance with the requirements of the Hazard Communication standard (29 CFR 1910.1200).

(k) MEDICAL SURVEILLANCE.

(1) General.

(i) The employer shall make medical surveillance available at no cost to the employee, and at a reasonable time and place, for all employees:

(A) Who are or may be occupationally exposed to chromium (VI) at or above the action level for 30 or more days a year;

(B) Experiencing signs or symptoms of the adverse health effects associated with chromium (VI) exposure; or

(C) Exposed in an emergency.

(ii) The employer shall assure that all medical examinations and procedures required by this section are performed by or under the supervision of a PLHCP.

(2) Frequency. The employer shall provide a medical examination:

(i) Within 30 days after initial assignment, unless the employee has received a chromium (VI) related medical examination that meets the requirements of this paragraph within the last twelve months;

(ii) Annually;

(iii) Within 30 days after a PLHCP's written medical opinion recommends an additional examination;

(iv) Whenever an employee shows signs or symptoms of the adverse health effects associated with chromium (VI) exposure;

(v) Within 30 days after exposure during an emergency which results in an uncontrolled release of chromium (VI); or

(vi) At the termination of employment, unless the last examination that satisfied the requirements of paragraph (k) of this section was less than six months prior to the date of termination.

(3) Contents of examination. A medical examination consists of:

(i) A medical and work history, with emphasis on: past, present, and anticipated future exposure to chromium (VI); any history of respiratory system dysfunction; any history of asthma, dermatitis, skin ulceration, or nasal septum perforation; and smoking status and history;

(ii) A physical examination of the skin and respiratory tract; and

(iii) Any additional tests deemed appropriate by the examining PLHCP.

(4) Information provided to the PLHCP. The employer shall ensure that the examining PLHCP has a copy of this standard, and shall provide the following information:

(i) A description of the affected employee's former, current, and anticipated duties as they relate to the employee's occupational exposure to chromium (VI);

(ii) The employee's former, current, and anticipated levels of occupational exposure to chromium (VI);

(iii) A description of any personal protective equipment used or to be used by the employee, including when and for how long the employee has used that equipment; and

(iv) Information from records of employment-related medical examinations previously provided to the affected employee, currently within the control of the employer.

(5) PLHCP's written medical opinion.

(i) The employer shall obtain a written medical opinion from the PLHCP, within 30 days for each medical examination performed on each employee, which contains:

(A) The PLHCP's opinion as to whether the employee has any detected medical condition(s) that would place the employee at increased risk of material impairment to health from further exposure to chromium (VI);

(B) Any recommended limitations upon the employee's exposure to chromium (VI) or upon the use of personal protective equipment such as respirators;

(C) A statement that the PLHCP has explained to the employee the results of the medical examination, including any medical conditions related to chromium (VI) exposure that require further evaluation or treatment, and any special provisions for use of protective clothing or equipment.

(ii) The PLHCP shall not reveal to the employer specific findings or diagnoses unrelated to occupational exposure to chromium (VI).

(iii) The employer shall provide a copy of the PLHCP's written medical opinion to the examined employee within two weeks after receiving it.

(l) COMMUNICATION OF CHROMIUM (VI) HAZARDS TO EMPLOYEES.

(1) General. In addition to the requirements of the Hazard Communication standard (29 CFR 1910.1200), employers shall comply with the following requirements.

(2) Employee information and training.

(i) The employer shall ensure that each employee can demonstrate knowledge of at least the following:

(A) The contents of this section; and

(B) The purpose and a description of the medical surveillance program required by paragraph (k) of this section.

(ii) The employer shall make a copy of this section readily available without cost to all affected employees.

(1) Air monitoring data.

(i) The employer shall maintain an accurate record of all air monitoring conducted to comply with the requirements of this section.

(ii) This record shall include at least the following information:

(A) The date of measurement for each sample taken;

(B) The operation involving exposure to chromium (VI) that is being monitored;

(C) Sampling and analytical methods used and evidence of their accuracy;

(D) Number, duration, and the results of samples taken;

(E) Type of personal protective equipment, such as respirators worn; and

(F) Name, social security number, and job classification of all employees represented by the monitoring, indicating which employees were actually monitored.

(iii) The employer shall ensure that exposure records are maintained and made available in accordance with 29 CFR 1910.1020.

(2) Historical monitoring data.

(i) Where the employer has relied on historical monitoring data to determine exposure to chromium (VI), the employer shall establish and maintain an accurate record of the historical monitoring data relied upon.

(ii) The record shall include information that reflects the following conditions:

(A) The data were collected using methods that meet the accuracy requirements of paragraph (d)(5) of this section;

(B) The processes and work practices that were in use when the historical monitoring data were obtained are essentially the same as those to be used during the job for which exposure is being determined;

(C) The characteristics of the chromium (VI) containing material being handled when the historical monitoring data were obtained are the same as those on the job for which exposure is being determined;

(D) Environmental conditions prevailing when the historical monitoring data were obtained are the same as those on the job for which exposure is being determined; and

(E) Other data relevant to the operations, materials, processing, or employee exposures covered by the exception.

(iii) The employer shall ensure that historical exposure records are maintained and made available in accordance with 29 CFR 1910.1020.

(3) Objective data.

(i) The employer shall maintain an accurate record of all objective data relied upon to comply with the requirements of this section.

(ii) This record shall include at least the following information:

(A) The chromium containing material in question;

(B) The source of the objective data;

(C) The testing protocol and results of testing, or analysis of the material for the release of chromium (VI);

(D) A description of the process, operation, or activity and how the data support the determination; and

(E) Other data relevant to the process, operation, activity, material, or employee exposures.

(iii) The employer shall ensure that objective data are maintained and made available in accordance with 29 CFR 1910.1020.

(4) Medical surveillance.

(i) The employer shall establish and maintain an accurate record for each employee covered by medical surveillance under paragraph (k) of this section.

(ii) The record shall include the following information about the employee:

(A) Name and social security number;

(B) A copy of the PLHCP's written opinions;

(C) A copy of the information provided to the PLHCP as required by paragraph (k)(4) of this section.

(iii) The employer shall ensure that medical records are maintained and made available in accordance with 29 CFR 1910.1020.

(1) For employers with 20 or more employees, all obligations of this section, except engineering controls required by paragraph (f) of this section, commence November 27, 2006.

(2) For employers with 19 or fewer employees, all obligations of this section, except engineering controls required by paragraph (f) of this section, commence May 30, 2007.

(3) For all employers, engineering controls required by paragraph (f) of this section shall be implemented no later than May 31, 2010.

(a) SCOPE.

(1) This standard applies to occupational exposures to chromium (VI) in all forms and compounds in shipyards, marine terminals, and longshoring, except:

(2) Exposures that occur in the application of pesticides regulated by the Environmental Protection Agency or another Federal government agency (e.g., the treatment of wood with preservatives);

(3) Exposures to portland cement; or

(4) Where the employer has objective data demonstrating that a material containing chromium or a specific process, operation, or activity involving chromium cannot release dusts, fumes, or mists of chromium (VI) in concentrations at or above 0.5 μg/m³ as an 8-hour time-weighted average (TWA) under any expected conditions of use.

(b) DEFINITIONS.

For the purposes of this section the following definitions apply:

Action level means a concentration of airborne chromium (VI) of 2.5 micrograms per cubic meter of air (2.5 μg/m³) calculated as an 8-hour time-weighted average (TWA).

Assistant Secretary means the Assistant Secretary of Labor for Occupational Safety and Health, U.S. Department of Labor, or designee.

Chromium (VI) [hexavalent chromium or Cr(VI)] means chromium with a valence of positive six, in any form and in any compound.

Director means the Director of the National Institute for Occupational Safety and Health (NIOSH), U.S. Department of Health and Human Services, or designee.

Emergency means any occurrence that results, or is likely to result, in an uncontrolled release of chromium (VI). If an incidental release of chromium (VI) can be controlled at the time of release by employees in the immediate release area, or by maintenance personnel, it is not an emergency.

Employee exposure means the exposure to airborne chromium (VI) that would occur if the employee were not using a respirator.

High-efficiency particulate air [HEPA] filter means a filter that is at least 99.97 percent efficient in removing mono-dispersed particles of 0.3 micrometers in diameter or larger.

Historical monitoring data means data from chromium (VI) monitoring conducted prior to May 30, 2006, obtained during work operations conducted under workplace conditions closely resembling the processes, types of material, control methods, work practices, and environmental conditions in the employer's current operations.

Objective data means information such as air monitoring data from industry-wide surveys or calculations based on the composition or chemical and physical properties of a substance demonstrating the employee exposure to chromium (VI) associated with a particular product or material or a specific process, operation, or activity. The data must reflect workplace conditions closely resembling the processes, types of material, control methods, work practices, and environmental conditions in the employer's current operations.

Physician or other licensed health care professional [PLHCP] is an individual whose legally permitted scope of practice (i.e., license, registration, or certification) allows him or her to independently provide or be delegated the responsibility to provide some or all of the particular health care services required by paragraph (i) of this section.

This section means this 1915.1026 chromium (VI) standard.

(c) PERMISSIBLE EXPOSURE LIMIT (PEL).

The employer shall ensure that no employee is exposed to an airborne concentration of chromium (VI) in excess of 5 micrograms per cubic meter of air (5 μg/m³), calculated as an 8-hour time-weighted average (TWA).

(d) EXPOSURE DETERMINATION.

(1) General. Each employer who has a workplace or work operation covered by this section shall determine the 8-hour TWA exposure for each employee exposed to chromium (VI). This determination shall be made in accordance with either paragraph (d)(2) or paragraph (d)(3) of this section.

(2) Scheduled monitoring option.

(i) The employer shall perform initial monitoring to determine the 8-hour TWA exposure for each employee on the basis of a sufficient number of personal breathing zone air samples to accurately characterize full shift exposure on each shift, for each job classification, in each work area. Where an employer does

representative sampling instead of sampling all employees in order to meet this requirement, the employer shall sample the employee(s) expected to have the highest chromium (VI) exposures.

(ii) If initial monitoring indicates that employee exposures are below the action level, the employer may discontinue monitoring for those employees whose exposures are represented by such monitoring.

(iii) If monitoring reveals employee exposures to be at or above the action level, the employer shall perform periodic monitoring at least every six months.

(iv) If monitoring reveals employee exposures to be above the PEL, the employer shall perform periodic monitoring at least every three months.

(v) If periodic monitoring indicates that employee exposures are below the action level, and the result is confirmed by the result of another monitoring taken at least seven days later, the employer may discontinue the monitoring for those employees whose exposures are represented by such monitoring.

(vi) The employer shall perform additional monitoring when there has been any change in the production process, raw materials, equipment, personnel, work practices, or control methods that may result in new or additional exposures to chromium (VI), or when the employer has any reason to believe that new or additional exposures have occurred.

(3) Performance-oriented option. The employer shall determine the 8-hour TWA exposure for each employee on the basis of any combination of air monitoring data, historical monitoring data, or objective data sufficient to accurately characterize employee exposure to chromium (VI).

(4) Employee notification of determination results.

(i) Where the exposure determination indicates that employee exposure exceeds the PEL, as soon as possible but not more than 5 working days later the employer shall either post the results in an appropriate location that is accessible to all affected employees or shall notify each affected employee individually in writing of the results.

(ii) Whenever the exposure determination indicates that employee exposure is above the PEL, the employer shall describe in the written notification the corrective action being taken to reduce employee exposure to or below the PEL.

(5) Accuracy of measurement. Where air monitoring is performed to comply with the requirements of

this section, the employer shall use a method of monitoring and analysis that can measure chromium (VI) to within an accuracy of plus or minus 25 percent (+/- 25%) and can produce accurate measurements to within a statistical confidence level of 95 percent for airborne concentrations at or above the action level.

(6) Observation of monitoring.

(i) Where air monitoring is performed to comply with the requirements of this section, the employer shall provide affected employees or their designated representatives an opportunity to observe any monitoring of employee exposure to chromium (VI).

(ii) When observation of monitoring requires entry into an area where the use of protective clothing or equipment is required, the employer shall provide the observer with clothing and equipment and shall assure that the observer uses such clothing and equipment and complies with all other applicable safety and health procedures.

(e) METHODS OF COMPLIANCE.

(1) Engineering and work practice controls.

(i) Except as permitted in paragraph (e)(1)(ii) of this section, the employer shall use engineering and work practice controls to reduce and maintain employee exposure to chromium (VI) to or below the PEL unless the employer can demonstrate that such controls are not feasible. Wherever feasible engineering and work practice controls are not sufficient to reduce employee exposure to or below the PEL, the employer shall use them to reduce employee exposure to the lowest levels achievable, and shall supplement them by the use of respiratory protection that complies with the requirements of paragraph (f) of this section.

(ii) Where the employer can demonstrate that a process or task does not result in any employee exposure to chromium (VI) above the PEL for 30 or more days per year (12 consecutive months), the requirement to implement engineering and work practice controls to achieve the PEL does not apply to that process or task.

(2) Prohibition of rotation. The employer shall not rotate employees to different jobs to achieve compliance with the PEL.

(f) RESPIRATORY PROTECTION.

(1) General. The employer shall provide respiratory protection for employees during:

(i) Periods necessary to install or implement feasible engineering and work practice controls;

(ii) Work operations, such as maintenance and repair activities, for which engineering and work practice controls are not feasible;

(iii) Work operations for which an employer has implemented all feasible engineering and work practice controls and such controls are not sufficient to reduce exposures to or below the PEL;

(iv) Work operations where employees are exposed above the PEL for fewer than 30 days per year, and the employer has elected not to implement engineering and work practice controls to achieve the PEL; or

(v) Emergencies.

(2) Respiratory protection program. Where respirator use is required by this section, the employer shall institute a respiratory protection program in accordance with 29 CFR 1910.134.

(g) PROTECTIVE WORK CLOTHING AND EQUIPMENT.

(1) Provision and use. Where a hazard is present or is likely to be present from skin or eye contact with chromium (VI), the employer shall provide appropriate personal protective clothing and equipment at no cost to employees, and shall ensure that employees use such clothing and equipment.

(2) Removal and storage.

(i) The employer shall ensure that employees remove all protective clothing and equipment contaminated with chromium (VI) at the end of the work shift or at the completion of their tasks involving chromium (VI) exposure, whichever comes first.

(ii) The employer shall ensure that no employee removes chromium (VI)-contaminated protective clothing or equipment from the workplace, except for those employees whose job it is to launder, clean, maintain, or dispose of such clothing or equipment.

(iii) When contaminated protective clothing or equipment is removed for laundering, cleaning, maintenance, or disposal, the employer shall ensure that it is stored and transported in sealed, impermeable bags or other closed, impermeable containers.

(iv) Bags or containers of contaminated protective clothing or equipment that are removed from change rooms for laundering, cleaning, maintenance, or disposal shall be labeled in accordance with the requirements of the Hazard Communication standard (29 CFR 1910.1200).

(3) Cleaning and replacement.

(i) The employer shall clean, launder, repair and replace all protective clothing and equipment required by this section as needed to maintain its effectiveness.

(ii) The employer shall prohibit the removal of chromium (VI) from protective clothing and equipment by blowing, shaking, or any other means that disperses chromium (VI) into the air or onto an employee's body.

(iii) The employer shall inform any person who launders or cleans protective clothing or equipment contaminated with chromium (VI) of the potentially harmful effects of exposure to chromium (VI) and that the clothing and equipment should be laundered or cleaned in a manner that minimizes skin or eye contact with chromium (VI) and effectively prevents the release of airborne chromium (VI) in excess of the PEL.

(h) HYGIENE AREAS AND PRACTICES.

(1) General. Where protective clothing and equipment is required, the employer shall provide change rooms in conformance with 29 CFR 1910.141. Where skin contact with chromium (VI) occurs, the employer shall provide washing facilities in conformance with 29 CFR 1915.97. Eating and drinking areas provided by the employer shall also be in conformance with §1915.97.

(2) Change rooms. The employer shall assure that change rooms are equipped with separate storage facilities for protective clothing and equipment and for street clothes, and that these facilities prevent cross-contamination.

(3) Washing facilities.

(i) The employer shall provide readily accessible washing facilities capable of removing chromium (VI) from the skin, and shall ensure that affected employees use these facilities when necessary.

(ii) The employer shall ensure that employees who have skin contact with chromium (VI) wash their hands and faces at the end of the work shift and prior to eating, drinking, smoking, chewing tobacco or gum, applying cosmetics, or using the toilet.

(4) Eating and drinking areas.

(i) Whenever the employer allows employees to consume food or beverages at a worksite where chromium (VI) is present, the employer shall ensure that eating and drinking areas and surfaces are maintained as free as practicable of chromium (VI).

(ii) The employer shall ensure that employees do not enter eating and drinking areas with protective work clothing or equipment unless surface chromium (VI) has been removed from the clothing and equip-

ment by methods that do not disperse chromium (VI) into the air or onto an employee's body.

(5) Prohibited activities. The employer shall ensure that employees do not eat, drink, smoke, chew tobacco or gum, or apply cosmetics in areas where skin or eye contact with chromium (VI) occurs; or carry the products associated with these activities, or store such products in these areas.

(i) MEDICAL SURVEILLANCE.

(1) General.

(i) The employer shall make medical surveillance available at no cost to the employee, and at a reasonable time and place, for all employees:

(A) Who are or may be occupationally exposed to chromium (VI) at or above the action level for 30 or more days a year;

(B) Experiencing signs or symptoms of the adverse health effects associated with chromium (VI) exposure; or

(C) Exposed in an emergency.

(ii) The employer shall assure that all medical examinations and procedures required by this section are performed by or under the supervision of a PLHCP.

(2) Frequency. The employer shall provide a medical examination:

(i) Within 30 days after initial assignment, unless the employee has received a chromium (VI) related medical examination that meets the requirements of this paragraph within the last twelve months;

(ii) Annually;

(iii) Within 30 days after a PLHCP's written medical opinion recommends an additional examination;

(iv) Whenever an employee shows signs or symptoms of the adverse health effects associated with chromium (VI) exposure;

(v) Within 30 days after exposure during an emergency which results in an uncontrolled release of chromium (VI); or

(vi) At the termination of employment, unless the last examination that satisfied the requirements of paragraph (i) of this section was less than six months prior to the date of termination.

(3) Contents of examination. A medical examination consists of:

(i) A medical and work history, with emphasis on: past, present, and anticipated future exposure to chromium (VI); any history of respiratory system dys-

function; any history of asthma, dermatitis, skin ulceration, or nasal septum perforation; and smoking status and history;

(ii) A physical examination of the skin and respiratory tract; and

(iii) Any additional tests deemed appropriate by the examining PLHCP.

(4) Information provided to the PLHCP. The employer shall ensure that the examining PLHCP has a copy of this standard, and shall provide the following information:

(i) A description of the affected employee's former, current, and anticipated duties as they relate to the employee's occupational exposure to chromium (VI);

(ii) The employee's former, current, and anticipated levels of occupational exposure to chromium (VI);

(iii) A description of any personal protective equipment used or to be used by the employee, including when and for how long the employee has used that equipment; and

(iv) Information from records of employment-related medical examinations previously provided to the affected employee, currently within the control of the employer.

(5) PLHCP's written medical opinion.

(i) The employer shall obtain a written medical opinion from the PLHCP, within 30 days for each medical examination performed on each employee, which contains:

(A) The PLHCP's opinion as to whether the employee has any detected medical condition(s) that would place the employee at increased risk of material impairment to health from further exposure to chromium (VI);

(B) Any recommended limitations upon the employee's exposure to chromium (VI) or upon the use of personal protective equipment such as respirators;

(C) A statement that the PLHCP has explained to the employee the results of the medical examination, including any medical conditions related to chromium (VI) exposure that require further evaluation or treatment, and any special provisions for use of protective clothing or equipment.

(ii) The PLHCP shall not reveal to the employer specific findings or diagnoses unrelated to occupational exposure to chromium (VI).

(iii) The employer shall provide a copy of the PLHCP's written medical opinion to the examined employee within two weeks after receiving it.

(1) General. In addition to the requirements of the Hazard Communication standard (29 CFR 1910.1200) employers shall comply with the following requirements.

(2) Employee information and training.

(i) The employer shall ensure that each employee can demonstrate knowledge of at least the following:

(A) The contents of this section; and

(B) The purpose and a description of the medical surveillance program required by paragraph (i) of this section.

(ii) The employer shall make a copy of this section readily available without cost to all affected employees.

(1) Air monitoring data.

(i) The employer shall maintain an accurate record of all air monitoring conducted to comply with the requirements of this section.

(ii) This record shall include at least the following information:

(A) The date of measurement for each sample taken;

(b) The operation involving exposure to chromium (VI) that is being monitored;

(C) Sampling and analytical methods used and evidence of their accuracy;

(D) Number, duration, and the results of samples taken;

(E) Type of personal protective equipment, such as respirators worn; and

(F) Name, social security number, and job classification of all employees represented by the monitoring, indicating which employees were actually monitored.

(iii) The employer shall ensure that exposure records are maintained and made available in accordance with 29 CFR 1910.1020.

(2) Historical monitoring data.

(i) Where the employer has relied on historical monitoring data to determine exposure to chromium (VI), the employer shall establish and maintain an accurate record of the historical monitoring data relied upon.

(ii) The record shall include information that reflects the following conditions:

(A) The data were collected using methods that meet the accuracy requirements of paragraph (d)(5) of this section;

(B) The processes and work practices that were in use when the historical monitoring data were obtained are essentially the same as those to be used during the job for which exposure is being determined;

(C) The characteristics of the chromium (VI) containing material being handled when the historical monitoring data were obtained are the same as those on the job for which exposure is being determined;

(D) Environmental conditions prevailing when the historical monitoring data were obtained are the same as those on the job for which exposure is being determined; and

(E) Other data relevant to the operations, materials, processing, or employee exposures covered by the exception.

(iii) The employer shall ensure that historical exposure records are maintained and made available in accordance with 29 CFR 1910.1020.

(3) Objective data.

(i) The employer shall maintain an accurate record of all objective data relied upon to comply with the requirements of this section.

(ii) This record shall include at least the following information:

(A) The chromium containing material in question;

(B) The source of the objective data;

(C) The testing protocol and results of testing, or analysis of the material for the release of chromium (VI);

(D) A description of the process, operation, or activity and how the data support the determination; and

(E) Other data relevant to the process, operation, activity, material, or employee exposures.

(iii) The employer shall ensure that objective data are maintained and made available in accordance with 29 CFR 1910.1020.

(4) Medical surveillance.

(i) The employer shall establish and maintain an accurate record for each employee covered by medical surveillance under paragraph (i) of this section.

(ii) The record shall include the following information about the employee:

(A) Name and social security number;

(B) A copy of the PLHCP's written opinions;

(C) A copy of the information provided to the PLHCP as required by paragraph (i)(4) of this section.

(iii) The employer shall ensure that medical records are maintained and made available in accordance with 29 CFR 1910.1020.

(l) DATES.

(1) For employers with 20 or more employees, all obligations of this section, except engineering controls required by paragraph (e) of this section, commence November 27, 2006.

(2) For employers with 19 or fewer employees, all obligations of this section, except engineering controls required by paragraph (e) of this section, commence May 30, 2007.

(3) For all employers, engineering controls required by paragraph (e) of this section shall be implemented no later than May 31, 2010.

(a) SCOPE.

(1) This standard applies to occupational exposures to chromium (VI) in all forms and compounds in construction, except:

(2) Exposures that occur in the application of pesticides regulated by the Environmental Protection Agency or another Federal government agency (e.g., the treatment of wood with preservatives);

(3) Exposures to portland cement; or

(4) Where the employer has objective data demonstrating that a material containing chromium or a specific process, operation, or activity involving chromium cannot release dusts, fumes, or mists of chromium (VI) in concentrations at or above 0.5 μg/m³ as an 8-hour time-weighted average (TWA) under any expected conditions of use.

(b) DEFINITIONS.

For the purposes of this section the following definitions apply:

Action level means a concentration of airborne chromium (VI) of 2.5 micrograms per cubic meter of air (2.5 μg/m³) calculated as an 8-hour time-weighted average (TWA).

Assistant Secretary means the Assistant Secretary of Labor for Occupational Safety and Health, U.S. Department of Labor, or designee.

Chromium (VI) [hexavalent chromium or Cr(VI)] means chromium with a valence of positive six, in any form and in any compound.

Director means the Director of the National Institute for Occupational Safety and Health (NIOSH), U.S. Department of Health and Human Services, or designee.

Emergency means any occurrence that results, or is likely to result, in an uncontrolled release of chromium (VI). If an incidental release of chromium (VI) can be controlled at the time of release by employees in the immediate release area, or by maintenance personnel, it is not an emergency.

Employee exposure means the exposure to airborne chromium (VI) that would occur if the employee were not using a respirator.

High-efficiency particulate air [HEPA] filter means a filter that is at least 99.97 percent efficient in removing mono-dispersed particles of 0.3 micrometers in diameter or larger.

Historical monitoring data means data from chromium (VI) monitoring conducted prior to May 30, 2006, obtained during work operations conducted under workplace conditions closely resembling the processes, types of material, control methods, work practices, and environmental conditions in the employer's current operations.

Objective data means information such as air monitoring data from industry-wide surveys or calculations based on the composition or chemical and physical properties of a substance demonstrating the employee exposure to chromium (VI) associated with a particular product or material or a specific process, operation, or activity. The data must reflect workplace conditions closely resembling the processes, types of material, control methods, work practices, and environmental conditions in the employer's current operations.

Physician or other licensed health care professional [PLHCP] is an individual whose legally permitted scope of practice (i.e., license, registration, or certification) allows him or her to independently provide or be delegated the responsibility to provide some or all of the particular health care services required by paragraph (i) of this section.

This section means this 1926.1126 chromium (VI) standard.

(c) PERMISSIBLE EXPOSURE LIMIT (PEL).

The employer shall ensure that no employee is exposed to an airborne concentration of chromium (VI) in excess of 5 micrograms per cubic meter of air (5 μg/m³), calculated as an 8-hour time-weighted average (TWA).

(d) EXPOSURE DETERMINATION.

(1) General. Each employer who has a workplace or work operation covered by this section shall determine the 8-hour TWA exposure for each employee exposed to chromium (VI). This determination shall be made in accordance with either paragraph (d)(2) or paragraph (d)(3) of this section.

(2) Scheduled monitoring option.

(i) The employer shall perform initial monitoring to determine the 8-hour TWA exposure for each employee on the basis of a sufficient number of personal breathing zone air samples to accurately characterize full shift exposure on each shift, for each job classifi-

cation, in each work area. Where an employer does representative sampling instead of sampling all employees in order to meet this requirement, the employer shall sample the employee(s) expected to have the highest chromium (VI) exposures.

(ii) If initial monitoring indicates that employee exposures are below the action level, the employer may discontinue monitoring for those employees whose exposures are represented by such monitoring.

(iii) If monitoring reveals employee exposures to be at or above the action level, the employer shall perform periodic monitoring at least every six months.

(iv) If monitoring reveals employee exposures to be above the PEL, the employer shall perform periodic monitoring at least every three months.

(v) If periodic monitoring indicates that employee exposures are below the action level, and the result is confirmed by the result of another monitoring taken at least seven days later, the employer may discontinue the monitoring for those employees whose exposures are represented by such monitoring.

(vi) The employer shall perform additional monitoring when there has been any change in the production process, raw materials, equipment, personnel, work practices, or control methods that may result in new or additional exposures to chromium (VI), or when the employer has any reason to believe that new or additional exposures have occurred.

(3) Performance-oriented option. The employer shall determine the 8-hour TWA exposure for each employee on the basis of any combination of air monitoring data, historical monitoring data, or objective data sufficient to accurately characterize employee exposure to chromium (VI).

(4) Employee notification of determination results.

(i) Where the exposure determination indicates that employee exposure exceeds the PEL, as soon as possible but not more than 5 working days later the employer shall either post the results in an appropriate location that is accessible to all affected employees or shall notify each affected employee individually in writing of the results.

(ii) Whenever the exposure determination indicates that employee exposure is above the PEL, the employer shall describe in the written notification the corrective action being taken to reduce employee exposure to or below the PEL.

(5) Accuracy of measurement. Where air monitoring is performed to comply with the requirements of this section, the employer shall use a method of monitoring and analysis that can measure chromium (VI) to within an accuracy of plus or minus 25 percent (+/- 25%) and can produce accurate measurements to within a statistical confidence level of 95 percent for airborne concentrations at or above the action level.

(6) Observation of monitoring.

(i) Where air monitoring is performed to comply with the requirements of this section, the employer shall provide affected employees or their designated representatives an opportunity to observe any monitoring of employee exposure to chromium (VI).

(ii) When observation of monitoring requires entry into an area where the use of protective clothing or equipment is required, the employer shall provide the observer with clothing and equipment and shall assure that the observer uses such clothing and equipment and complies with all other applicable safety and health procedures.

(e) METHODS OF COMPLIANCE.

(1) Engineering and work practice controls.

(i) Except as permitted in paragraph (e)(1)(ii) of this section, the employer shall use engineering and work practice controls to reduce and maintain employee exposure to chromium (VI) to or below the PEL unless the employer can demonstrate that such controls are not feasible. Wherever feasible engineering and work practice controls are not sufficient to reduce employee exposure to or below the PEL, the employer shall use them to reduce employee exposure to the lowest levels achievable, and shall supplement them by the use of respiratory protection that complies with the requirements of paragraph (f) of this section.

(ii) Where the employer can demonstrate that a process or task does not result in any employee exposure to chromium (VI) above the PEL for 30 or more days per year (12 consecutive months), the requirement to implement engineering and work practice controls to achieve the PEL does not apply to that process or task.

(2) Prohibition of rotation. The employer shall not rotate employees to different jobs to achieve compliance with the PEL.

(f) RESPIRATORY PROTECTION.

(1) General. The employer shall provide respiratory protection for employees during:

(i) Periods necessary to install or implement feasible engineering and work practice controls;

(ii) Work operations, such as maintenance and repair activities, for which engineering and work practice controls are not feasible;

(iii) Work operations for which an employer has implemented all feasible engineering and work practice controls and such controls are not sufficient to reduce exposures to or below the PEL;

(iv) Work operations where employees are exposed above the PEL for fewer than 30 days per year, and the employer has elected not to implement engineering and work practice controls to achieve the PEL; or

(v) Emergencies.

(2) Respiratory protection program. Where respirator use is required by this section, the employer shall institute a respiratory protection program in accordance with 29 CFR 1910.134.

(g) PROTECTIVE WORK CLOTHING AND EQUIPMENT.

(1) Provision and use. Where a hazard is present or is likely to be present from skin or eye contact with chromium (VI), the employer shall provide appropriate personal protective clothing and equipment at no cost to employees, and shall ensure that employees use such clothing and equipment.

(2) Removal and storage.

(i) The employer shall ensure that employees remove all protective clothing and equipment contaminated with chromium (VI) at the end of the work shift or at the completion of their tasks involving chromium (VI) exposure, whichever comes first.

(ii) The employer shall ensure that no employee removes chromium (VI)-contaminated protective clothing or equipment from the workplace, except for those employees whose job it is to launder, clean, maintain, or dispose of such clothing or equipment.

(iii) When contaminated protective clothing or equipment is removed for laundering, cleaning, maintenance, or disposal, the employer shall ensure that it is stored and transported in sealed, impermeable bags or other closed, impermeable containers.

(iv) Bags or containers of contaminated protective clothing or equipment that are removed from change rooms for laundering, cleaning, maintenance, or disposal shall be labeled in accordance with the requirements of the Hazard Communication standard (29 CFR 1910.1200).

(3) Cleaning and replacement.

(i) The employer shall clean, launder, repair and replace all protective clothing and equipment required by this section as needed to maintain its effectiveness.

(ii) The employer shall prohibit the removal of chromium (VI) from protective clothing and equipment by blowing, shaking, or any other means that disperses chromium (VI) into the air or onto an employee's body.

(iii) The employer shall inform any person who launders or cleans protective clothing or equipment contaminated with chromium (VI) of the potentially harmful effects of exposure to chromium (VI) and that the clothing and equipment should be laundered or cleaned in a manner that minimizes skin or eye contact with chromium (VI) and effectively prevents the release of airborne chromium (VI) in excess of the PEL.

(h) HYGIENE AREAS AND PRACTICES.

(1) General. Where protective clothing and equipment is required, the employer shall provide change rooms in conformance with 29 CFR 1926.51. Where skin contact with chromium (VI) occurs, the employer shall provide washing facilities in conformance with 29 CFR 1926.51. Eating and drinking areas provided by the employer shall also be in conformance with §1926.51.

(2) Change rooms. The employer shall assure that change rooms are equipped with separate storage facilities for protective clothing and equipment and for street clothes, and that these facilities prevent cross-contamination.

(3) Washing facilities.

(i) The employer shall provide readily accessible washing facilities capable of removing chromium (VI) from the skin, and shall ensure that affected employees use these facilities when necessary.

(ii) The employer shall ensure that employees who have skin contact with chromium (VI) wash their hands and faces at the end of the work shift and prior to eating, drinking, smoking, chewing tobacco or gum, applying cosmetics, or using the toilet.

(4) Eating and drinking areas.

(i) Whenever the employer allows employees to consume food or beverages at a worksite where chromium (VI) is present, the employer shall ensure that eating and drinking areas and surfaces are maintained as free as practicable of chromium (VI).

(ii) The employer shall ensure that employees do not enter eating and drinking areas with protective work clothing or equipment unless surface chromium (VI) has been removed from the clothing and equip-

ment by methods that do not disperse chromium (VI) into the air or onto an employee's body.

(5) Prohibited activities. The employer shall ensure that employees do not eat, drink, smoke, chew tobacco or gum, or apply cosmetics in areas where skin or eye contact with chromium (VI) occurs; or carry the products associated with these activities, or store such products in these areas.

(i) MEDICAL SURVEILLANCE.

(1) General.

(i) The employer shall make medical surveillance available at no cost to the employee, and at a reasonable time and place, for all employees:

(A) Who are or may be occupationally exposed to chromium (VI) at or above the action level for 30 or more days a year;

(B) Experiencing signs or symptoms of the adverse health effects associated with chromium (VI) exposure; or

(C) Exposed in an emergency.

(ii) The employer shall assure that all medical examinations and procedures required by this section are performed by or under the supervision of a PLHCP.

(2) Frequency. The employer shall provide a medical examination:

(i) Within 30 days after initial assignment, unless the employee has received a chromium (VI) related medical examination that meets the requirements of this paragraph within the last twelve months;

(ii) Annually;

(iii) Within 30 days after a PLHCP's written medical opinion recommends an additional examination;

(iv) Whenever an employee shows signs or symptoms of the adverse health effects associated with chromium (VI) exposure;

(v) Within 30 days after exposure during an emergency which results in an uncontrolled release of chromium (VI); or

(vi) At the termination of employment, unless the last examination that satisfied the requirements of paragraph (i) of this section was less than six months prior to the date of termination.

(3) Contents of examination. A medical examination consists of:

(i) A medical and work history, with emphasis on: past, present, and anticipated future exposure to chromium (VI); any history of respiratory system dys-

function; any history of asthma, dermatitis, skin ulceration, or nasal septum perforation; and smoking status and history;

(ii) A physical examination of the skin and respiratory tract; and

(iii) Any additional tests deemed appropriate by the examining PLHCP.

(4) Information provided to the PLHCP. The employer shall ensure that the examining PLHCP has a copy of this standard, and shall provide the following information:

(i) A description of the affected employee's former, current, and anticipated duties as they relate to the employee's occupational exposure to chromium (VI);

(ii) The employee's former, current, and anticipated levels of occupational exposure to chromium (VI);

(iii) A description of any personal protective equipment used or to be used by the employee, including when and for how long the employee has used that equipment; and

(iv) Information from records of employment-related medical examinations previously provided to the affected employee, currently within the control of the employer.

(5) PLHCP's written medical opinion.

(i) The employer shall obtain a written medical opinion from the PLHCP, within 30 days for each medical examination performed on each employee, which contains:

(A) The PLHCP's opinion as to whether the employee has any detected medical condition(s) that would place the employee at increased risk of material impairment to health from further exposure to chromium (VI);

(B) Any recommended limitations upon the employee's exposure to chromium (VI) or upon the use of personal protective equipment such as respirators;

(C) A statement that the PLHCP has explained to the employee the results of the medical examination, including any medical conditions related to chromium (VI) exposure that require further evaluation or treatment, and any special provisions for use of protective clothing or equipment.

(ii) The PLHCP shall not reveal to the employer specific findings or diagnoses unrelated to occupational exposure to chromium (VI).

(iii) The employer shall provide a copy of the PLHCP's written medical opinion to the examined employee within two weeks after receiving it.

(1) General. In addition to the requirements of the Hazard Communication standard (29 CFR 1910.1200) employers shall comply with the following requirements.

(2) Employee information and training.

(i) The employer shall ensure that each employee can demonstrate knowledge of at least the following:

(A) The contents of this section; and

(B) The purpose and a description of the medical surveillance program required by paragraph (i) of this section.

(ii) The employer shall make a copy of this section readily available without cost to all affected employees.

(1) Air monitoring data.

(i) The employer shall maintain an accurate record of all air monitoring conducted to comply with the requirements of this section.

(ii) This record shall include at least the following information:

(A) The date of measurement for each sample taken;

(B) The operation involving exposure to chromium (VI) that is being monitored;

(C) Sampling and analytical methods used and evidence of their accuracy;

(D) Number, duration, and the results of samples taken;

(E) Type of personal protective equipment, such as respirators worn; and

(F) Name, social security number, and job classification of all employees represented by the monitoring, indicating which employees were actually monitored.

(iii) The employer shall ensure that exposure records are maintained and made available in accordance with 29 CFR 1910.1020.

(2) Historical monitoring data.

(i) Where the employer has relied on historical monitoring data to determine exposure to chromium (VI), the employer shall establish and maintain an accurate record of the historical monitoring data relied upon.

(ii) The record shall include information that reflects the following conditions:

(A) The data were collected using methods that meet the accuracy requirements of paragraph (d)(5) of this section;

(B) The processes and work practices that were in use when the historical monitoring data were obtained are essentially the same as those to be used during the job for which exposure is being determined;

(C) The characteristics of the chromium (VI) containing material being handled when the historical monitoring data were obtained are the same as those on the job for which exposure is being determined;

(D) Environmental conditions prevailing when the historical monitoring data were obtained are the same as those on the job for which exposure is being determined; and

(E) Other data relevant to the operations, materials, processing, or employee exposures covered by the exception.

(iii) The employer shall ensure that historical exposure records are maintained and made available in accordance with 29 CFR 1910.1020.

(3) Objective data.

(i) The employer shall maintain an accurate record of all objective data relied upon to comply with the requirements of this section.

(ii) This record shall include at least the following information:

(A) The chromium containing material in question;

(B) The source of the objective data;

(C) The testing protocol and results of testing, or analysis of the material for the release of chromium (VI);

(D) A description of the process, operation, or activity and how the data support the determination; and

(E) Other data relevant to the process, operation, activity, material, or employee exposures.

(iii) The employer shall ensure that objective data are maintained and made available in accordance with 29 CFR 1910.1020.

(4) Medical surveillance.

(i) The employer shall establish and maintain an accurate record for each employee covered by medical surveillance under paragraph (i) of this section.

(ii) The record shall include the following informa-

tion about the employee:

(A) Name and social security number;

(B) A copy of the PLHCP's written opinions;

(C) A copy of the information provided to the PLHCP as required by paragraph (i)(4) of this section.

(iii) The employer shall ensure that medical records are maintained and made available in accordance with 29 CFR 1910.1020.

(l) DATES.

(1) For employers with 20 or more employees, all obligations of this section, except engineering controls required by paragraph (e) of this section, commence November 27, 2006.

(2) For employers with 19 or fewer employees, all obligations of this section, except engineering controls required by paragraph (e) of this section, commence May 30, 2007.

(3) For all employers, engineering controls required by paragraph (e) of this section shall be implemented no later than May 31, 2010.

This appendix identifies industry operations or processes associated with occupational exposure to Cr(VI). For each of these sectors, a brief description of potential sources of Cr(VI) exposure is presented.

ELECTROPLATING

Exposures to Cr(VI) can occur in hard chrome plating, decorative chrome plating, and anodizing operations. Cr(VI) exposures can also occur in chromium conversion coating operations. Chromium conversion is not an electroplating process but often takes place in electroplating shops.

Employee exposures to Cr(VI) during chrome electroplating and chromium conversion coating operations occur as a result of the formation of chromate-containing mists and aerosols that are released from the chromate/chromic acid bath. Mists and aerosols containing Cr(VI) are released from hydrogen bubbles that form and burst during the electroplating process. They may also be released when platers add or remove parts from the bath. Helpers may also be exposed to Cr(VI) when adding chemical agents to the bath or when disposing of chromate-containing wastewater.

WELDING

Exposures to Cr(VI) can occur when welding or cutting operations are performed on stainless steel, other metals containing Cr(VI), or surfaces coated with Cr(VI) paint. Welding on carbon steel in confined or enclosed spaces may also result in Cr(VI) exposures.

Employee exposure to Cr(VI) is expected to increase as the chromium content of the base material increases. Therefore, one would expect that exposures would tend to be higher for welding on stainless steel (10 to 24% chromium) versus welding on carbon steel (generally 3% chromium or less). However, there are other factors that can greatly affect exposures to Cr(VI) during welding operations. These factors include: the type of welding process used [Flux Cored Arc Welding (FCAW), Shielded Metal Arc Welding (SMAW), and Gas Metal Arc Welding (GMAW) generate the highest fume levels while Tungsten Inert Gas (TIG) and Submerged Arc Welding (SAW) generate lower levels]; the environment where welding is taking place (exposures are lower in open spaces versus confined or other enclosed spaces); and the composition of the filler metal, flux material or shielding gas used, which can affect the amount of fume generated. Other factors can also influence the amount of fume generated. For example, increasing the welding current and voltage tend to increase the amount of welding fume generated.

In carbon steel welding, most exposures to Cr(VI) are usually well below the PEL due to the low percentage of chromium metal in carbon steel. Ninety percent (90%) of the carbon steel produced has only trace amounts of chromium. Ten percent (10%) of the carbon steel produced contains up to 3% chromium. Carbon steel welders in confined spaces may experience elevated Cr(VI) exposures, though most exposures will be below the PEL.

Welding a stanchion (Photo courtesy of Bath Iron Works).

PAINTING

Paints and coatings that contain Cr(VI) are applied to a wide variety of structures and products. Cr(VI) paints and coatings are also removed from structures and products in many situations. Both of these scenarios may result in employee exposure to Cr(VI).

Aerospace

In the aerospace industry, employees may be exposed to Cr(VI) during painting of aircraft (exterior or interior) or aircraft parts, and during removal of chromate-based coatings. The primary Cr(VI)-containing product used is strontium chromate primer, which is used as a corrosion inhibitor on metal surfaces (particularly alu-

Occupational Safety and Health Administration

minum). To a lesser extent, zinc chromate is used in primers for corrosion protection for some products. Employees may be exposed to Cr(VI)-containing aerosols during spray painting. Spray painters may also be exposed during abrasive blasting, sanding, and grinding tasks. Assemblers may be exposed to Cr(VI) when performing drilling, grinding, and sanding tasks.

Automotive

Cr(VI)-containing paints and primers are used in some automotive refinishing facilities. Lead chromate pigments are also still used in some top coats and pre-treatments, and Cr(VI) coatings are still widely used for corrosion control in the undercoat. Spray painters and technicians can be exposed to Cr(VI) when performing surface preparation tasks such as sanding, grinding, and abrasive blasting as well as during spray painting activities.

Coil Coating

Coil coating is the application of surface coatings containing Cr(VI) to the surface of metal coil. In this process, a coil (roll) of uncoated sheet metal is coated on one or both sides. The coated metal strip is then nor-mally rewound into a coil and packaged for ship-ment or further processing. Coil coating tasks that can result in exposure to Cr(VI) include coating transfer, coating machine operation, metal feeding operations, roll-winding operations, and maintenance operations. Maintenance personnel have the potential for dermal exposure when handling the coil coatings. Operators can be exposed to Cr(VI) while performing tasks for maintaining the viscosity of the coating, maintaining the desired coating thickness, and cleaning of the rollers.

Construction and Shipyards

Prior to the 1970s, exposed steel surfaces such as bridges, water towers, and industrial buildings were often painted with Cr(VI) primers and paints colored with chromate-based pigments. During the late 1970s and early 1980s, the use of Cr(VI) compounds for these applications began to decline. Cr(VI)-containing paints and coatings are now used very rarely in the construction industry. Similarly, Cr(VI) paints and primers were once commonly used on ships and other marine vessels but are now used infrequently.

Cr(VI) exposures can occur when removing old paint by abrasive blasting (or infrequently by sanding, chipping, or grinding) from structures or vessels that have been previously painted with Cr(VI)-containing paints or primers. Exposures can also occur in those limited situations where spray painting of Cr(VI)-containing primers and paints still occurs and during cleanup activities.

Traffic Painting

Cr(VI)-containing paints are also used in some traffic painting operations. There are two types of traffic painting operations: road striping and painting of roadside curbs and traffic islands. Both involve the use of Cr(VI)-containing paint that is diluted with toluene (as necessary) during painting operations. Employees are potentially exposed to Cr(VI) during this mixing task. Painting of roadside curbs and traffic islands typically involves use of a hand-held spray line, which also involves potential Cr(VI) exposure.

PRODUCERS OF CHROMATES AND RELATED CHEMICALS FROM CHROMITE ORE

This industry includes facilities that produce sodium chromate/sodium dichromate (SDC) and other related compounds from chromite ore. Employees are ex-posed during production of SDC and other related compounds because all of the compounds produced are Cr(VI) compounds. Process operators, packaging employees, and maintenance employees have the greatest potential Cr(VI) exposure.

CHROMATE PIGMENT PRODUCERS

This industry includes facilities that produce chromi-um pigments from Cr(VI) compounds such as sodium chromate and sodium bichromate. Employees who are potentially exposed to Cr(VI) include those who perform drying, blending, or packaging operations; strike tank operators; maintenance employees; labor-ers; laboratory technicians; wastewater treatment operators; managers and supervisors; proprietary process operators; and dispersion operators.

The highest exposures to Cr(VI) occur when em-ployees handle chromate materials in the dry form, which can generate airborne particles. The activities that have the potential for the highest exposures are drying, blending, and packaging. Maintenance em-ployees are exposed to residual dust that deposits on process equipment as well as elevated background Cr(VI) levels in the process area. Wastewater treat-ment operators are exposed during collection of sys-tem samples and are also exposed to elevated background Cr(VI) levels. Proprietary process operators are exposed to Cr(VI) from inhaling the dried material that accumulates on conveyor surfaces. Strike tank operators are subject to increased background levels of exposure from Cr(VI) generated during other processes.

CHROMATED COPPER ARSENATE (CCA) PRODUCERS

This industry includes facilities that produce chromated copper arsenate (CCA), which is used as a wood preservative. The activities with the potential for highest exposures are dumping drums of chromic acid (flakes) into a reactor and rinsing the inside of rail tank cars after chromic acid is unloaded. Employees may also be exposed to residual dust that settles on surfaces in warehouse areas.

CHROMIUM CATALYST PRODUCERS

Exposures to Cr(VI) in chromium catalyst production occur as a result of using Cr(VI)-based raw materials (e.g., sodium bichromate), intermediate products (e.g., sodium chromate), and final products (e.g., ammonium dichromate, cadmium chromate, calcium dichromate, chromyl chloride, copper chromate, copper dichromate, magnesium dichromate, nickel chromate, silver chromate, tetramin copper (II) chromate). Employees potentially exposed to Cr(VI) include warehouse operators, maintenance personnel, screening operators, quality control inspectors, dry-mix operators, process control operators, control room operators, forming operators, team leaders, and floor persons.

Wet processors are potentially exposed to Cr(VI)-containing dust and mist while mixing chemicals to form a precipitate known as "striking", while removing filter cake from a filter press, when loading and operating a dryer, and while adding Cr(VI)-containing raw materials as a dry solid or liquid solution to a mixing tank. Dry process operators are potentially exposed to Cr(VI) when loading the calciner, when operating the forming machines, and when operating the catalyst tablet forming machines. Dry mixing operators are potentially exposed to Cr(VI) during the manual transfer of Cr(VI)-containing raw materials. Screening operators are exposed to dust as they manually load the screening machine hoppers and stand next to the flat deck screen as the catalyst product is screened. Solid waste handlers have the potential for exposure to Cr(VI) dust as they load and handle plastic bags with Cr(VI) contaminated waste.

PAINT AND COATINGS PRODUCERS

Cr(VI) exposures in the paint and coatings production industry result from the use of chromate pigments. Exposure to Cr(VI) is primarily from contact with dry chromate pigment powders. Exposures are expected to be lower at paint and coating production plants that receive the chromate pigments in slurry form (i.e., in 300 gallon tote tanks or 30-55 gallon drums).

The three primary categories of employees exposed to Cr(VI) are batch makers, packagers, and shippers/receivers. Batch makers have the highest potential exposures while opening bags of chromate pigment, handling the bags, and dumping the material. Shippers/receivers can also be exposed while handling bags containing pigments.

PRINTING AND INK PRODUCERS

In the past, lead chromate pigments were commonly used in the manufacture of some printing inks. The pigments used include chrome yellow, chrome orange, and molybdate orange. Currently, lead chromate pigments are seldom used in printing inks. Screenprinting ink production is the only sector of this industry that uses chromate-based inks. Lead chromate ink is used primarily for silk-screen printing on outdoor billboards, posters and signs. Lead chromate ink is also used in fabric silk screening applications.

The primary exposures in this industry occur when dry lead chromate pigments are weighed and added to the mixer. The batch mixing operation has the potential for the highest Cr(VI) exposures. Batch weighers are exposed to Cr(VI) while weighing the Cr(VI)-containing pigments, adding ingredients to the mixer, mixing the product, and disposing of the empty bags. Airborne exposures to mill operators, utility employees, and maintenance employees are greatly reduced because by the time they get involved in the process the pigments are no longer in powder form.

PLASTIC COLORANT PRODUCERS AND USERS

This industry includes firms that produce Cr(VI)-containing colorants for use in plastics and companies that use dry Cr(VI)-containing pigments or pigment blends in the manufacture of plastic products. Employees who are potentially exposed to Cr(VI) include dry color handlers, wet mill operators, dry color blenders/packagers, and production supervisors.

Employee exposures to Cr(VI) in the plastic colorant producers and users industry occur when employees handle chromate materials in the dry form,

which generates fine airborne dust particles. The highest exposures occur in the production activities that involve blending and packaging of Cr(VI)-containing dry color colorants (single pigments or pigment blends).

PLATING MIXTURE PRODUCERS

This industry produces plating mixtures to be used in the electroplating process. Cr(VI) exposures in this industry arise from the use of chromic acid as a primary ingredient in the production of plating mixtures. Plating mixtures are formulated as powders or crystals and are sold to facilities in the metal finishing industry. Employees in the industry that are potentially exposed to Cr(VI) include:

- Mixer/blender operators- dry chrome process
- Mixer/blender operators- liquid chrome process
- Laboratory chemists

FERROCHROMIUM PRODUCERS

This industry uses ferrochromium to produce stainless and heat resisting steels, welding rods, and corrosion-resistant high strength materials (i.e., superalloys). Ferrochromium is produced in high and low carbon forms. High carbon ferrochromium contains 50% to 70% chromium and 4% to 10% carbon. Low carbon ferrochromium contains 65% to 75% chromium and less than 1% carbon.

Many employees in this industry are potentially exposed to Cr(VI) including leach operators, ager operators, lower cell room operators, cell assemblers, cell operators, plate hookers, plate strippers, and mill operators. Leach operators are primarily exposed to Cr(VI) that escapes when the hatch of the anolyte reduction solution tank is opened to collect samples and when making adjustments to the anolyte-reduction process equipment. Ager operators are primarily exposed to Cr(VI) through collection of samples from the ager tanks, and through exposure to chromium solution mist that escapes from open-top ager tanks. Cell assemblers, cell operators, and plate hookers are exposed to Cr(VI) from the anolyte solution mist that escapes from the cell surface area that is not covered or controlled by existing local exhaust ventilation (LEV). The lower cell room operator is exposed to background levels of Cr(VI) that escape from the electrolytic cells during normal operation, and during cell-cleaning operations. Plate strippers are exposed to background levels of Cr(VI) from the chromic acid bath due to their close proximity to the plate stripping station.

STEEL MILLS

In this industry, chromium is used in steels as an alloying agent to improve hardness and resistance to corrosion, tarnish, rust, extreme temperature, bacterial buildup and wear. Cr(VI) alloys are added to the furnace just before tapping, or to the ladle as the molten metal is tapped.

The primary sources of Cr(VI) in this industry include chromium fumes from furnace operations, tapping, and teeming (pouring), and chromium-containing particulates from surface conditioning operations. Background Cr(VI) levels in the steel mill contribute to the low exposures of many employees (e.g., rolling mill operators, continuous casting operators) who do not have direct contact with molten metal or significant dust-emitting sources. Employees in the iron and steel producing industry who are potentially exposed to Cr(VI) include raw material handlers, furnace operators, furnace helper/laborers, crane operators, continuous-casting operators, rolling mill operators, steel conditioning operators, and welders.

IRON AND STEEL FOUNDRIES

This industry includes companies that produce cast metal products from steel and other metals and metal alloys. The primary source of Cr(VI) exposures in iron and steel foundries is the Cr(VI) fumes generated when chromium is melted as part of the pour or when grinding or welding the finished part. These exposures occur during the following operations:

- Furnace operation activities (e.g., making alloy additions, removing slag, tapping furnaces into ladles, pouring molten metal into molds)
- Torch cutting and gouging
- Welding

Employees in the iron and steel foundry industry who are potentially exposed to Cr(VI) include molders, furnace operators, crane operators, pourers, shake-out and abrasive blasting operators, torch cutter/gougers, welders, grinding operators, and laborers. Furnace operators, crane operators, molders, pourers and laborers are exposed to background Cr(VI) from electric arc furnace operation, pouring, grinding and welding. Grinder operators are exposed to Cr(VI) containing fume and dust that is generated in the grinding process and escapes capture by the ventilation system.

Filling molds in a foundry (Photo courtesy of the National Institute for Occupational Safety and Health (NIOSH)).

CHROMIUM DYE PRODUCERS

Cr(VI) is used in the production of several different dyes to improve wash fastness, allowing the color of the dyed wool not to change, bleed or stain other fabrics during textile processing, wear, or washing. Exposure to Cr(VI) in the dye production process may occur when bags of chromic acid flakes or other chromate chemicals are emptied into vessels to be mixed with other chemicals, and during packaging. Employees such as color makers, drying/blending/packaging operators, maintenance employees, laborers, laboratory technicians, wastewater treatment operators, and managers/supervisors are potentially exposed to Cr(VI). The highest employee exposures to Cr(VI) in the chromate dye production industry occur when employees handle chromate materials in the dry form such as drying, blending, and packaging, which generates fine airborne dust particles.

CHROMIUM SULFATE PRODUCERS

Chromium sulfate is primarily used in chrome leather tanning. While chromium sulfate is a trivalent chromium (Cr(III)) compound, employee exposures occur because it is made by reducing sodium bichromate and chromate (two Cr(VI) compounds). Chromate sulfate production can result in exposures to Cr(VI) from processes that include the reduction of sodium bichromate with organic compounds such as molasses or sugar in the presence of sulfuric acid, and the reduction of sodium bichromate with sulfur dioxide. Employees who are exposed to Cr(VI) include reactor operators and railcar operators.

CHEMICAL DISTRIBUTORS

Chemical distributors purchase or import chemicals in bulk and re-sell the chemicals to various chemical manufacturers or industries for use in their operations. The two major Cr(VI) compounds that are sold by chemical distributors are sodium dichromate and chromic acid.

Employees may be exposed to Cr(VI) during the storage, handling, transportation, and disposal of Cr(VI) compounds. Exposures to Cr(VI) during chemical distribution occur when bags containing chromium chemicals are being repackaged. A slight potential for exposure to Cr(VI) exists during transportation of Cr(VI) compounds; chromate dust accumulated on the bags may be disturbed, creating a potential for exposure to Cr(VI).

TEXTILE DYEING

This industry includes companies involved in the dyeing of textile fabrics. Sources of Cr(VI) in textile dyeing include Cr(VI)-containing dyes and use of chromates as mordants. Blenders, dyers, and maintenance employees may be exposed to Cr(VI).

PRINTING

This industry includes companies that use Cr(VI)-containing inks in their printing processes. The Cr(VI)-based inks are colored inks containing pigments from lead chromate or lead molybdate. The majority of exposures to Cr(VI) occur in commercial screen printing. Printers, mixers, and shippers are potentially exposed to Cr(VI).

PRODUCERS OF GLASS PRODUCTS

This industry includes the producers of colored glass and other glass products such as fiberglass continuous glass filaments. The raw materials which are used for colored glass production contain Cr(VI). Cr(VI) is not used as an ingredient in other glass products, but the refractories in the furnaces used in glass production may contain trivalent chromium (Cr(III)). During heating, the Cr(III) is oxidized to Cr(VI), resulting in potential employee exposure to Cr(VI) at these plants.

In colored glass production, lab employees, batch mixers, and furnace employees are potentially exposed to Cr(VI). For other glass production, employees who are potentially exposed to Cr(VI) include batch operators, furnace operators, electrostatic precipitator/baghouse operators, forehearth operators, hot end repair operators, and furnace rebuild operators.

OSHA
Occupational Safety and
Health Administration

Furnace employees in fiberglass typically have slightly higher exposures than furnace employees in continuous filament plants because the furnaces have openings above the channels and forehearths to cool the glass while continuous filament furnaces are closed. Also, hot end repair employees in continuous filament production are expected to have higher exposures because of the need to regularly replace bushings at the end of the forehearth.

Weighing Cr(VI) pigment for colored glass production (Photo courtesy of the National Institute for Occupational Safety and Health (NIOSH)).

CHROMIUM CATALYST USERS

Cr(VI)-containing catalysts are used in processes such as the production of plastics and polymers, in chemical synthesis, and gas production. In some processes, Cr(III) catalysts are activated by heat and converted by oxidation to Cr(VI). Catalysts are usually sold in powder form or in specific shapes such as small pellets, and are packaged in bags or drums. Pellets generate less dust than powders during packaging and handling.

The tasks of loading and unloading Cr(VI)-containing catalysts into and out of catalyst process reactors and holding vessels present the greatest potential for Cr(VI) exposure among chromium catalyst users. Employees who perform these tasks include catalyst service company field technicians who load and unload catalyst and process operators who load catalysts into process vessels prior to activation of the catalyst.

PRODUCERS OF REFRACTORY BRICK

This industry includes companies that produce refractory brick from other materials. Refractories are either clay or non-clay. Certain non-clay refractories contain chromium, primarily chromite ore (Cr(III)). In addition, although basic refractories are produced from Cr(III) based ores, small quantities of chromic acid (Cr(VI)) may be added to produce specialty products. Sometimes Cr(III) is mixed with salvaged material which can contain Cr(VI). Employees potentially exposed to Cr(VI) are cleaners, crusher operators, pressmen, batchmen, mold fillers, brick loaders, grinder operators, saw operators, and engineering interns. These employees have potential Cr(VI) exposure because of the physical form (e.g., powder) of the Cr(VI)-containing chemicals that are handled.

WOODWORKING

Chromated copper arsenate (CCA) is one of the major chemicals used to treat wood to prevent biodegradation, and Cr(VI) is used in the formulation of CCA. Although treatment of wood with preservatives is exempt from the scope of the Cr(VI) standards because pesticide applications are regulated by the Environmental Protection Agency, downstream uses of Cr(VI)-treated wood are covered by the standards. Employees in many downstream woodworking industries such as lumber yards, carpentry shops, and landscaping handle, cut, saw, sand, and paint CCA treated lumber. Carpenters and carpenter helpers are the primary groups exposed to Cr(VI) from woodworking. The principal source of airborne exposures is the dust created during wood processing activities such as cutting, drilling, and sanding, and is not CCA leaching out of the treated wood.

EPA requires that, as of 2003, CCA treated wood cannot be used to construct play structures, decks, picnic tables, landscaping timbers, patios, boardwalks, and residential fencing. CAA treated wood will continue to be produced for permitted uses, such as salt water use, highway construction, utility poles, and pilings.

SOLID WASTE INCINERATION

Exposure to Cr(VI) in waste incineration results from the thermal destruction of chromium-containing products discarded by consumers and industry. Employees potentially exposed to Cr(VI) include laborers, shredder/heavy equipment operators, maintenance and helpers, boiler operators and assistant operators, maintenance electricians, and truck operators (ash hauling). The job of shredder/heavy equipment operators is unique to facilities which shred or process refuse prior to delivery to the incineration unit. Tasks involving periodic incinerator clean-out are a major source of exposure.

NON-FERROUS SUPERALLOY PRODUCERS AND USERS OF CHROMIUM

This group includes firms that produce or use nonferrous-based high performance alloys. These alloys are known as "superalloys" because they have better performance at high temperatures (1500 to 2000 degrees Fahrenheit) than conventional alloys. These alloys also withstand relatively severe mechanical stresses and typically have higher surface stability than conventional alloys. Nickel or cobalt, not iron, are the primary metal constituents of these alloys. The nickel-based alloys can contain 10% to 30% elemental chromium. Cobalt-based alloys generally contain even higher concentrations of elemental chromium.

In this industry the primary source of exposure to Cr(VI) is from fumes generated from the molten alloy during furnace/refining operations (particularly during the electroslag remelt process) and from welding activities. In these situations the chromium is not originally hexavalent, but the high temperatures involved in the process result in oxidation that converts the chromium to a hexavalent state. Employees potentially exposed to Cr(VI) include melt specialists, reclaim weigh operators, electric arc furnace operators, vacuum induction melt/air induction melt furnace operators, crane operators, refining unit operators, floor persons, welders, inert screeners, machine operators, laboratory technicians, and maintenance employees.

CONSTRUCTION

This sector includes general building contractors and operative builders, heavy construction, and special trade contractors. In addition to those employees potentially exposed to Cr(VI) during painting and surface preparation, welding and thermal cutting, and woodworking operations involving chromated copper arsenate (CCA)-treated lumber, construction employees may be exposed to Cr(VI) during several other operations.

Refractory Restoration and Maintenance

Recycled refractory bricks are used as salvage material in manufacturing new refractories. Although most chromium in refractories is trivalent, the Cr(III) can be converted to Cr(VI) under the conditions found in the ovens. Recycled refractory bricks are often contaminated with yellow crystals. These crystals are thought to be sodium chromate due to the prevalence of sodium in the glassmaking process. The salvage material can contain high Cr(VI) concentrations. Employees repairing and restoring refractory bricks are exposed to this material.

Hazardous Waste Site Work

Employees can be exposed to Cr(VI) at hazardous waste sites in the course of sampling the environment at the site to determine the extent of contamination and through remediation activities. Remediation activities may include soil excavation, groundwater pumping, and subsequent treatment using such techniques as incineration or stabilization. Even sites which are not legally considered hazardous waste sites can be sources of Cr(VI). Examples are parks where chromate chemical production waste was used as fill and diking material.

Industrial Rehabilitation and Maintenance

Construction employees are routinely involved in maintenance and rehabilitation work at industrial facilities. The employees may come into contact with Cr(VI) when employed at sites where chromium products are manufactured, processed, or otherwise present.

A. OSHA AREA OFFICES

Alabama
U.S. Department of Labor - OSHA
Vestavia Village, 2047 Canyon Road
Birmingham, AL 35216-1981
(205) 731-1534

U.S. Department of Labor - OSHA
1141 Montlimar Drive, Suite 1006
Mobile, AL 36609
(251) 441-6131

Alaska
U.S. Department of Labor - OSHA
301 W. Northern Lights Blvd, Suite 407
Anchorage, AK 99503
(907) 271-5152

Arizona
U.S. Department of Labor - OSHA
230 North 1st Avenue, Suite 202
Phoenix, AZ 85003
(602) 640-2348

Arkansas
U.S. Department of Labor - OSHA
TCBY Building, Suite 450
425 West Capitol Avenue
Little Rock, AR 72201
(501) 224-1841

California
U.S. Department of Labor - OSHA
5675 Ruffin Road, Suite 330
San Diego, CA 92123
(415) 975-4310

Colorado
U.S. Department of Labor - OSHA
1391 Speer Boulevard, Suite 210
Denver, CO 80204-2552
(303) 844-5285

U.S. Department of Labor - OSHA
7935 East Prentice Avenue, Suite 209
Greenwood Village, CO 80111-2714
(303) 843-4500

Connecticut
U.S. Department of Labor - OSHA
1057 Broad Street, Fourth Floor
Bridgeport, CT 06604
(203) 579-5581

U.S. Department of Labor - OSHA
Federal Building
450 Main Street, Room 613
Hartford, CT 06103
(860) 240-3152

Delaware
U.S. Department of Labor - OSHA
Caleb Boggs Federal Building
844 N King Street, Room 2209
Wilmington, DE 19801-3319
(302) 573-6518

Florida
U.S. Department of Labor - OSHA
8040 Peters Road, Building H-100
Fort Lauderdale, FL 33324
(954) 424-0242

U.S. Department of Labor - OSHA
Ribault Building, Suite 227
1851 Executive Center Drive
Jacksonville, FL 32207
(904) 232-2895

U.S. Department of Labor - OSHA
5807 Breckenridge Parkway, Suite A
Tampa, FL 33610-4249
(813) 626 1177

Georgia
U.S. Department of Labor - OSHA
450 Mall Boulevard, Suite J
Savannah, GA 31419
(912) 652-4393

U.S. Department of Labor - OSHA
2400 Herodian Way, Suite 250
Smyrna, GA 30080-2968
(770) 984-8700

U.S. Department of Labor - OSHA
LaVista Perimeter Office Park
2183 N. Lake Parkway
Building 7 - Suite 110
Tucker, GA 30084-4154
(770) 493-6644/6742/8419

Idaho
U.S. Department of Labor - OSHA
1150 North Curtis Road, Suite 201
Boise, ID 83706
(208) 321-2960

Illinois
U.S. Department of Labor - OSHA
1600 167th Street, Suite 9
Calumet City, IL 60409
(708) 891-3800

U.S. Department of Labor - OSHA
O'hara Plaza
701 Lee Street, Suite #950
Des Plaines, IL 60016
(847) 803-4800

U.S. Department of Labor - OSHA
11 Executive Drive, Suite 11
Fairview Heights, IL 62208
(618) 632-8612

U.S. Department of Labor - OSHA
365 Smoke Tree Business Park
North Aurora, IL 60542
(630) 896-8700

U.S. Department of Labor - OSHA
2918 West Willow Knolls Road
Peoria, IL 61614
(309) 671-7033

Indiana
U.S. Department of Labor - OSHA
46 East Ohio Street, Room 453
Indianapolis, IN 46204
(317) 226-7290

Iowa
U.S. Department of Labor - OSHA
210 Walnut Street, Room 815
Des Moines, IA 50309
(515) 284-4794

Kansas
U.S. Department of Labor - OSHA
217 W. 3rd Street North
Room #400
Wichita, KS 67202
(316) 269-6644

Kentucky
U.S. Department of Labor - OSHA
John C. Watts Federal Building
330 W. Broadway, Room 108
Frankfort, KY 40601-1922
(502) 227-7024

Louisiana
U.S. Department of Labor - OSHA
9100 Bluebonnet Centre Boulevard
Suite 201
Baton Rouge, LA 70809
(225) 298-5458

Maine
U.S. Department of Labor - OSHA
202 Harlow Street, Room 211
Bangor, ME 04401
(207) 941-8177

U.S. Department of Labor - OSHA
West Tower
100 Middle Street, Suite 410 West
Portland, ME 04101
(207) 626-9160

Maryland
U.S. Department of Labor - OSHA
1099 Winterson Road, Suite 140
Linthicum, MD 21090-2218
(410) 865-2055/2056

Massachusetts
U.S. Department of Labor - OSHA
639 Granite Street, 4th Floor
Braintree, MA 02184
(617) 565-6924

U.S. Department of Labor - OSHA
Valley Office Park
13 Branch Street
Methuen, MA 01844
(617) 565-8110

U.S. Department of Labor - OSHA
1441 Main Street, Room 550
Springfield, MA 01103-1493
(413) 785-0123

Michigan
U.S. Department of Labor - OSHA
801 South Waverly Road, Suite 306
Lansing, MI 48917-4200
(517) 487-4996

Minnesota
U.S. Department of Labor - OSHA
Minneapolis, MN 55415
*closed – please contact Eau Claire Wisconsin office at
(715) 832-9019

Mississippi
U.S. Department of Labor - OSHA
3780 I-55 North, Suite 210
Jackson, MS 39211-6323
(601) 965-4606

Missouri
U.S. Department of Labor - OSHA
6200 Connecticut Avenue, Suite 100
Kansas City, MO 64120
(816) 483-9531

U.S. Department of Labor - OSHA
911 Washington Avenue, Room 420
St. Louis, MO 63101
(314) 425-4249

Montana
U.S. Department of Labor - OSHA
2900 4th Avenue North, Suite 303
Billings, MT 59101
(406) 247-7494

Nebraska
U.S. Department of Labor - OSHA
Overland - Wolf Building
6910 Pacific Street, Room 100
Omaha, NE 68106
(402) 553-0171

Nevada
U.S. Department of Labor - OSHA
705 North Plaza, Room 204
Carson City, NV 89701
(775) 885-6963

New Hampshire
U.S. Department of Labor - OSHA
279 Pleasant Street, Suite 201
Concord, NH 03301
(603) 225-1580

New Jersey
U.S. Department of Labor - OSHA
1030 St. Georges Avenue
Plaza 35, Suite 205
Avenel, NJ 07001
(732) 750-3270

U.S. Department of Labor - OSHA
500 Route 17 South, 2nd Floor
Hasbrouck Heights, NJ 07604
(201) 288-1700

U.S. Department of Labor - OSHA
Marlton Executive Park, Building 2
701 Route 73 South, Suite 120
Marlton, NJ 08053
(856) 757-5181

U.S. Department of Labor - OSHA
299 Cherry Hill Road, Suite 304
Parsippany, NJ 07054
(973) 263-1003

New York
U.S. Department of Labor - OSHA
401 New Karner Road, Suite 300
Albany, NY 12205-3809
(518) 464-4338

U.S. Department of Labor - OSHA
42-40 Bell Boulevard
Bayside, NY 11361
(718) 279-9060

U.S. Department of Labor - OSHA
5360 Genesee Street
Bowmansville, NY 14026
(716) 551-3053

U.S. Department of Labor - OSHA
201 Varick Street - Room #646
New York, NY 10014
(212) 620-3200

U.S. Department of Labor - OSHA
3300 Vickery Road
North Syracuse, NY 13212
(315) 451-0808

U.S. Department of Labor - OSHA
660 White Plains Road, 4th Floor
Tarrytown, NY 10591-5107
(914) 524-7510

U.S. Department of Labor - OSHA
1400 Old Country Road, Room 208
Westbury, NY 11590
(516) 334-3344

North Carolina
U.S. Department of Labor - OSHA
Century Station Federal Office Building
300 Fayetteville Street Mall, Room 438
Raleigh, NC 27601-9998
(919) 856-4770

North Dakota
U.S. Department of Labor - OSHA
1640 East Capitol Avenue
Bismark, ND 58501
(701) 250-4521

Ohio
U.S. Department of Labor - OSHA
36 Triangle Park Drive
Cincinnati, OH 45246
(513) 841-4132

U.S. Department of Labor - OSHA
Federal Office Building
1240 East 9th Street, Room 899
Cleveland, OH 44199
(216) 522-3818

U.S. Department of Labor - OSHA
Federal Office Building
200 North High Street, Room 620
Columbus, OH 43215
(614) 469-5582

U.S. Department of Labor - OSHA
420 Madison Avenue
Suite 600
Toledo, OH 43604
(419) 259-7542

Oklahoma
U.S. Department of Labor - OSHA
55 North Robinson, Suite 315
Oklahoma City, OK 73102-9237
(405) 278-9560

Oregon
U.S. Department of Labor, OSHA
Federal Office Building
1220 Southwest 3rd Avenue, Room 640
Portland, OR 97204
(503) 326-2251

Pennsylvania
U.S. Department of Labor - OSHA
850 North 5th Street
Allentown, PA 18102
(610) 776-0592

U.S. Department of Labor - OSHA
3939 West Ridge Road, Suite B12
Erie, PA 16506-1887
(814) 833-5758

U.S. Department of Labor - OSHA
Progress Plaza
49 North Progress Avenue
Harrisburg, PA 17109
(717) 782-3902

U.S. Department of Labor - OSHA
U.S. Custom House, Room 242
Second and Chestnut Streets
Philadelphia, PA 19106-2902
(215) 597-4955

U.S. Department of Labor - OSHA
Federal Office Building
1000 Liberty Avenue, Room 1428
Pittsburgh, PA 15222-4101
(412) 395-4903

U.S. Department of Labor - OSHA
Steigmaier
7 North Wilkes-Barre Boulevard, Suite 410
Wilkes-Barre, PA 18702-350
(570) 826-6538

Puerto Rico
U.S. Department of Labor - OSHA
Triple SSS Plaza Building
1510 F. D. Roosevelt Avenue, Suite 5B
Guaynabo, PR 00968
(787) 277-1560

Rhode Island
U.S. Department of Labor - OSHA
Federal Office Building
380 Westminster Mall, Room 543
Providence, RI 02903
(401) 528-4669

South Carolina
U.S. Department of Labor - OSHA
1835 Assembly Street, Room 1468
Columbia, SC 29201-2453
(803) 765-5904

Tennessee
U.S. Department of Labor - OSHA
2002 Richard Jones Road, Suite C-205
Nashville, TN 37215-2809
(615) 781-5423

Texas
U.S. Department of Labor - OSHA
1033 La Posada Drive, Suite 375
Austin, TX 78752-3832
(512) 374-0271

U.S. Department of Labor - OSHA
Wilson Plaza
606 N. Carancahua, Suite 700
Corpus Christi, TX 78476
(361) 888-3420

U.S. Department of Labor - OSHA
8344 East R.L. Thornton Freeway, Suite 420
Dallas, TX 75228
(214) 320-2400 (2558)

U.S. Department of Labor - OSHA
700 E San Antonio St.
Room C-408
El Paso, TX 79901
(915) 534-6251

U.S. Department of Labor - OSHA
North Starr II, Suite 302
8713 Airport Freeway
Fort Worth, TX 76180-7610
(817) 428-2470 (485-7647)

U.S. Department of Labor - OSHA
507 N. Sam Houston Pky., Suite 400
Houston, TX 77060
(281) 591-2438 (2787)

U.S. Department of Labor - OSHA
17625 El Camino Real, Suite 400
Houston, TX   77058
(281) 286-0583/0584 (5922)

U.S. Department of Labor - OSHA
Federal Office Building
1205 Texas Avenue, Room 806
Lubbock, TX 79401
(806) 472-7681 (7685)

Utah
U.S. Depaartment of Labor - OSHA
160 E 300 South
Heber-Wells Building
P. O. Box 146650
Salt Lake City, UT 84114-6650
(801) 233-4900

Virginia
U.S. Department of Labor - OSHA
Federal Office Building
200 Granby Street, Room 614
Norfolk, VA 23510
(757) 441-3820

Washington
U.S. Department of Labor - OSHA
505 106th Avenue, NE, Suite 302
Bellevue, WA 98004
(425) 450-5438

West Virginia
U.S. Department of Labor - OSHA
405 Capitol Street
Suite 407
Charleston, WV 25301
(304) 347-5937

Wisconsin
U.S. Department of Labor - OSHA
1648 Tri Parkway
Appleton, WI 54914

(920) 734-4521
U.S. Department of Labor - OSHA
1310 West Clairmont Avenue
Eau Claire, WI 54701
(715) 832-9019

U.S. Department of Labor - OSHA
4802 E. Broadway
Madison, WI 53716
(608) 441-5388

U.S. Department of Labor - OSHA
Henry S. Reuss Building
310 W. Wisconsin Ave, Suite 1180
Milwaukee, WI 53203
(414) 297-3315

Region I
(CT*, ME, MA, NH, RI, VT*)
JFK Federal Building, Room E340
Boston, Massachusetts 02203
Boston, MA 02203
(617) 565-9860

Region II
(NJ*, NY*, PR*, VI*)
201 Varick Street, Room 670
New York, NY 10014
(212) 337-2378

Region III
(DE, DC, MD*, PA*, VA*, WV)
The Curtis Center
170 S. Independence Mall West
Suite 740 West
Philadelphia, PA 19106-3309
(215) 861-4900

Region IV
(AL, FL, GA, KY*, MS, NC*, SC*, TN*)
Atlanta Federal Center
61 Forsyth Street SW, Room 6T50
Atlanta, GA 30303
(404) 562-2300

Region V
(IL, IN*, MI*, MN*, OH, WI)
230 South Dearborn Street,
Room 3244
Chicago, IL 60604
(312) 353-2220

Region VI
(AR, LA, NM*, OK, TX)
525 Griffin Street, Room 602
Dallas, TX 75202
(214) 767-4731 or 4736 x224

Region VII
(IA*, KS, MO, NE)
City Center Square
1100 Main Street, Suite 800
Kansas City, MO 64105
(816) 426-5861

Region VIII
(CO, MT, ND, SD, UT*, WY*)
1999 Broadway, Suite 1690
PO Box 46550
Denver, CO 80202-5716
(720) 264-6550

Region IX
(American Samoa, AZ*, CA*, HI, NV*, Northern Mariana Islands)
71 Stevenson Street, Room 420
San Francisco, CA 94105
(415) 975-4310

Region X
(AK*, ID, OR*, WA*)
1111 Third Avenue, Suite 715
Seattle, WA 98101-3212
(206) 553-5930

*These states and territories operate their own OHSA-approved job safety and health programs (Connecticut, New Jersey, New York, and Virgin Islands plans cover public employees only). States with approved programs must have a standard that is identical to, or at least as effective as, the federal standard.

OSHA
Occupational Safety and
Health Administration

Alaska Department of Labor and Workforce Development
P.O. Box 21149
1111 W. 8th Street, Room 306
Juneau, Alaska 99802-1149
Commissioner (907) 465-2700 Fax: (907) 465-2784
Director (907) 465-4855 Fax: (907) 465-6012

Industrial Commission of Arizona
800 W. Washington
Phoenix, Arizona 85007-2922
Director, ICA(602) 542-4411 Fax: (602) 542-1614
Program Director (602) 542-5795 Fax: (602) 542-1614

California Department of Industrial Relations
1515 Clay Street, Suite 1901
Oakland, California 94612
Acting Director (415) 703-5050 Fax:(415) 703-5059
Acting Chief, Cal/OSHA (510) 286-7000
FAX (510) 286-7038
Deputy Chief, Cal/OSHA (714) 939-8093
FAX (714) 939-8094

Connecticut Department of Labor
200 Folly Brook Boulevard
Wethersfield, Connecticut 06109
Commissioner (860) 566-5123 Fax: (860) 566-1520
Conn-OSHA
38 Wolcott Hill Road
Wethersfield, Connecticut 06109
Director (860) 263-6900 Fax: (860) 263-6940

Hawaii Department of Labor and Industrial Relations
830 Punchbowl Street
Honolulu, Hawaii 96813
Director (808) 586-8844 Fax: (808) 586-9099

Indiana Department of Labor
State Office Building
402 West Washington Street, Room W195
Indianapolis, Indiana 46204-2751
Commissioner (317) 232-2378 Fax: (317) 233-3790
Deputy Commissioner (317) 233-3605
Fax: (317) 233-3790

Iowa Division of Labor
1000 E. Grand Avenue
Des Moines, Iowa 50319-0209
Commissioner (515) 281-3447 Fax: (515) 281-4698
Administrator (515) 281-3469 Fax: (515) 281-7995

Kentucky Department of Labor
1047 U.S. Highway 127 South, Suite 4
Frankfort, Kentucky 40601
Commissioner (502) 564-3070 Fax: (502) 564-5387
Executive Director, Office of Occupational Safety & Health
(502) 564-3070 Fax: (502) 564-1682

Maryland Division of Labor and Industry
Department of Labor, Licensing and Regulation
1100 North Eutaw Street, Room 613
Baltimore, Maryland 21201-2206
Commissioner (410) 767-2241 Fax: (410) 767-2986
Assistant Commissioner, MOSH (410) 767-2190
Fax: (410) 333-7747

Michigan Department of Labor and Economic Growth
Robert Swanson, Acting Director
Michigan Occupational Safety and Health Administration
P.O. Box 30643
Lansing, MI 48909-8143
Director (517) 322-1814 Fax: (517) 322-1775
Deputy Director for Enforcement (517) 322-1817
Fax: (517) 322-1775

Minnesota Department of Labor and Industry
443 Lafayette Road
St. Paul, Minnesota 55155
Commissioner (651) 284-5010 Fax: (651) 282-5405
Assistant Commissioner (651) 284-5371
Fax: (651) 282-2527
Administrative Director, OSHA Management Team
(651) 284-5372 Fax: (651) 297-2527

Nevada Division of Industrial Relations
400 West King Street, Suite 400
Carson City, Nevada 89703
Administrator (775) 684-7260 Fax: (775) 687-6305
Occupational Safety and Health Enforcement
Section (OSHES)
1301 N. Green Valley Parkway
Henderson, Nevada 89014
Chief Administrative Officer (702) 486-9168
Fax: (702) 486-9020
[Las Vegas (702) 687-5240]

New Jersey Department of Labor and Workforce Development
Office of Public Employees Occupational Safety & Health
(PEOSH)
1 John Fitch Plaza
P.O. Box 386
Trenton, NJ 08625-0386
Acting Commissioner (609) 292-2975 Fax: (609) 633-9271
Assistant Commissioner (609) 292-2313 Fax: (609) 695-1314
Director, PSOSH (609) 292-0501 Fax: (609) 292-3749
Director, Occupational Health Service (609) 984-1843
Fax: (609) 984-0849

New Mexico Environment Department
1190 St. Francis Drive, Suite 4050
P.O. Box 26110
Santa Fe, New Mexico 87502
Secretary (505) 827-2850 Fax: (505) 827-2836
Bureau Chief (505) 476-8700 Fax: (505) 476-8734

New York Department of Labor
New York Public Employee Safety and Health Program
State Office Campus Building 12, Room 158
Albany, New York 12240
Commissioner (518) 457-2741 Fax: (518) 457-6908
Director, Division of Safety and Health
(518) 457-3518 Fax: (518) 457-1519
Program Manager (518) 457-1263 Fax: (518) 457-5545

North Carolina Department of Labor
4 West Edenton Street
Raleigh, North Carolina 27601-1092
Commissioner (919) 733-0359 Fax: (919) 733-1092
Deputy Commissioner, OSH Director (919) 807-2861
Fax: (919) 807-2855
OSH Assistant Director (919) 807-2863 Fax: (919) 807-2856

Oregon Occupational Safety and Health Division
Department of Consumer and Business Services
350 Winter Street, NE, Room 430
Salem, Oregon 97301-3882
Administrator (503) 378-3272 Fax: (503) 947-7461
Deputy Administrator (503) 378-3272 Fax: (503) 947-7461
Special Assistant for Federal & External Affairs
(503) 378-3272 Fax: (503) 947-7461

Puerto Rico Department of Labor
Prudencio Rivera Martínez Building
505 Muñoz Rivera Avenue
Hato Rey, Puerto Rico 00918
Secretary (787) 754-2119 Fax: (787) 753-9550
Assistant Secretary for Occupational Safety and Health
(787) 756-1100 / (787) 754-2171 Fax: (787) 767-6051

South Carolina Department of Labor, Licensing, and Regulation
Koger Office Park, Kingstree Building
110 Centerview Drive
PO Box 11329
Columbia, South Carolina 29211
Director (803) 896-4300 Fax: (803) 896-4393
Administrator (803) 896-7665 Fax: (803) 896-7670
Office of Voluntary Programs (803) 896-7744
Fax: (803) 896-7750

Tennessee Department of Labor and Workforce Development
710 James Robertson Parkway
Nashville, Tennessee 37243-0659
Commissioner (615) 741-2582 Fax: (615) 741-5078
Program Director (615) 741-2793 Fax: (615) 741-3325

Utah Labor Commission
160 East 300 South, 3rd Floor
PO Box 146650
Salt Lake City, Utah 84114-6650
Commissioner (801) 530-6901 Fax: (801) 530-7906
Administrator (801) 530-6898 Fax: (801) 530-6390

Vermont Department of Labor
National Life Building - Drawer 20
Montpelier, Vermont 05620-3401
Commissioner (802) 828-2288 Fax: (802) 828-2748
VOSHA Compliance Program Manager (802) 828-2765
Fax: (802) 828-2195

Virgin Islands Department of Labor
3012 Golden Rock
Christiansted, St. Croix, Virgin Islands 00820-4660
Commissioner (340) 773-1994 Fax: (340) 773-1858
Assistant Commissioner (340) 772-1315
Fax: (340) 772-4323
Program Director (340) 772-1315 Fax: (340) 772-4323

Virginia Department of Labor and Industry
Powers-Taylor Building
13 South 13th Street
Richmond, Virginia 23219
Commissioner (804) 786-2377 Fax: (804) 371-6524
Director, Safety Compliance, VOSHA (804) 786-2391 Fax:
(804) 371-6524
Director, Office of Legal Support (804) 786-9873 Fax: (804)
786-8418

Washington Department of Labor and Industries
General Administration Building
PO Box 44001
Olympia, Washington 98504-4001
7273 Linderson Way SW
Tumwater, WA 98501-5414
Director (360) 902-4200 Fax: (360) 902-4202
Assistant Director [PO Box 44600]
(360) 902-5495 Fax: (360) 902-5529
Program Manager, Federal-State Operations
[PO Box 44600]
(360) 902-5430 Fax: (360) 902-5529

Wyoming Department of Employment
Workers' Safety and Compensation Division
Cheyenne Business Center
1510 East Pershing Boulevard
Cheyenne, Wyoming 82002
Administrator (307) 777-7700 Fax: (307) 777-5524
OSHA Program Manager (307) 777-7786 Fax: (307) 777-3646

Note: the Connecticut, New Jersey, New York, and Virgin Islands plans cover public sector (State and Local Government) employment only.

Occupational Safety and Health Administration

D. OSHA CONSULTATION PROJECT DIRECTORY

(For the most current contact information, please go to: http://www.osha.gov/dcsp/smallbusiness/consult_directory.html)

Alabama
Safe State Program
University of Alabama
432 Martha Parham West
Box 870388
Tuscaloosa, Alabama 35487
(205) 348-3033
Director
FAX: (205) 348-3049

Alaska
Consultation Section
ADOL/AKOSH
3301 Eagle Street-Suite 305
Anchorage, Alaska 99503-4149

Mailing:
Post Office Box 107022
Anchorage, Alaska 99510
(907) 269-4957
Chief of Consultation and Training
FAX: (907) 269-4950

Arizona
Consultation and Training
Div. of Occupational Safety & Health
Industrial Commission of Arizona
2675 East Broadway Road
Tucson, Arizona 85716
(520) 628-5478
Project Manager
FAX: (520) 322-8008

Arkansas
OSHA Consultation
Arkansas Department of Labor
10421 West Markham
Little Rock, Arkansas 72205
(501) 682-4522
Labor Safety Admin.
FAX: (501) 682-4532

California
CAL/OSHA Consultation Service
2424 Arden Way, Suite 485
Sacramento, California 95825
(916) 263-5765
Program Manager
FAX: (916) 263-5760

Colorado
Colorado State University
Health & Safety Consultation
Department of Environmental and Radiological Health Sciences
1681 Campus Delivery
Fort Collins, Colorado 80523-1681
(970) 491-6151
Project Manager
FAX: (970) 491-7778

Connecticut
Connecticut Department of Labor
Div. of Occupational Safety & Health
38 Wolcott Hill Road
Wethersfield, Connecticut 06109
(860) 263-6901
7(c)(1) Project Manager
FAX: (860) 263-6940

Delaware
Delaware Department of Labor
Occupational Safety &Health
Division of Industrial Affairs
4425 North Market Street
Wilmington, Delaware 19802
(302) 761-8198
Deputy Director
FAX: (302) 761-6602

District of Columbia
Office of Occupational Safety and Health
D. C. Dept of Employment Services
64 New York Avenue, N.E., Room 2106
Washington, D.C. 20002
(202) 671-1800
Safety Supervisor
FAX: (202) 673-2380

Florida
University of South Florida
Department of Environmental and Occupational Health
College of Public Health
13201 Bruce B. Downs Boulevard
MDC 56
Tampa, Florida 33612-3805
(813) 927-5347
Associate Director
FAX: (813) 974-8270
(866) 273-1105

Georgia
21(d) Onsite Consultation Program
Georgia Institute of Technology
430 10th Street, NW
North Building
Atlanta, Georgia 30332-0837
(404) 894-8276
Program Manager
FAX: (404) 894-8275

Guam
Guam Department of Labor
OSHA On-site Consultation Division
414 W. Soledad Avenue, 8th Floor
GCIC Building
Hagatna, Guam 96910

Mailing:
Post Office Box 9970
Tamuning, Guam 96931
(671) 475-7069
Project Manager
FAX: (671) 475-7070

Hawaii
HI DOL & Industrial Relations
Consultation and Training Branch
830 Punchbowl Street-Room 423
Honolulu, Hawaii 96813
(808) 586-9078
OSH Business Safety Facilitator
FAX: (808) 586-9099

Idaho
Idaho OSHA Consultation Program
Boise State University
1910 University Drive
M.S. 1835-College of Health Sciences
Boise, Idaho 83725-1835
(208) 426-3795
Project Manager
FAX: (208) 426-2199

Illinois
Illinois On-site Consultation
Department of Commerce &
Economic Opportunity (DCEO)
Division of Industrial Services
State of Illinois Center, Suite 3-400
100 West Randolph Street
Chicago, Illinois 60601
(312) 814-2337, (800)972-4216
Project Manager
FAX: (312) 814-7238

Indiana
Indiana Department of Labor
INSafe – On-Site Consultation Program
402 West Washington Street
Room W195
Indianapolis, Indiana 46204-2287
(317) 232-2655
Deputy Commissioner
FAX: (317) 232-3790

Iowa
Iowa Workforce Development
Division of Labor Services
Bureau of Consultation and Education
1000 East Grand Avenue
Des Moines, Iowa 50319
(515) 281-7629
Project Manager
FAX: (515) 281-5522

Kansas
Kansas Department of Labor
Kansas Consultation Project
800 SW Jackson Street-Suite 1500
Topeka, Kansas 66612-1227
(785) 296-6325
Project Manager
FAX: (785) 296-1775

Kentucky
Division of Education and Training
Kentucky OSH Program
Kentucky Labor Cabinet
1047 U.S. Highway 127, South
Suite 4
Frankfort, Kentucky 40601
(502) 564-3070
Director
FAX: (505) 827-4422

Louisiana
21(d) Consultation Program
Louisiana Department of Labor
1001 North 23rd Street, Rm. 421 Annex
Baton Rouge, Louisiana 70804

Mailing:
Post Office Box 94094
Baton Rouge, Louisiana 70804-9094
(225) 342-9601
Consultation Project Manager
FAX: (225) 342-5158

Maine
Maine Bureau of Labor Standards
Workplace Safety & Health Division
#45 State House Station
Augusta, Maine 04333-0045
(207) 624-6400
Director
FAX: (207) 624-6449

Maryland
MOSH Consultation Services
Montgomery Park Business Center
1827 Washington Boulevard
Baltimore, Maryland 21230
(410) 537-4500
Project Manager
FAX: (410) 537-4518

Massachusetts
MA Department of Labor
Division of Occupational Safety
1001 Watertown Street
West Newton, Massachusetts 02465
(617) 969-7177
Project Manager
FAX: (617) 727-4581

Michigan
Department of Labor and Economic Growth
Bureau of Safety & Occupational Regulation
Consultation, Education and Training
7150 Harris Drive, Post Office Box 30643
Lansing, Michigan 48909-8413
(517) 322-1809
Assistant Chief
FAX: (517) 322-1374

Minnesota
MN Department of Labor & Industry
Workplace Safety Consultation Division
443 LaFayette Road North
Saint Paul, Minnesota 55155
(651) 284-5060
Consultation Director
FAX: (651) 284-5739

Mississippi
Mississippi State University
Center for Safety and Health
2151 Highway 18, Suite B
Brandon, Mississippi 39042
(601) 825-0783
Director
FAX: (601) 825-6609

Missouri
Onsite Consultation Program
Division of Labor Standards
Dept. of Labor & Industrial Relations
3315 West Truman Boulevard
Post Office Box 449
Jefferson City, Missouri 65102
(573) 751-3403
Project Manager
FAX: (573) 751-3721

Montana
Department of Labor & Industry
Occupational Safety & Health Bureau
1625 11th Avenue
Post Office Box 1728
Helena, Montana 59601
(406) 444-6418
Project Manager
FAX: (406) 444-9396

Nebraska
Nebraska Workforce Development
Office of Safety and Labor Standards
State Office Building, Lower Level
Post Office Box 95024
301 Centennial Mall, South
Lincoln, Nebraska 68509-5024
(402) 471-4717
Project Manager
FAX: (402) 471-5039

Nevada
Safety, Consultation & Training Section
Division of Industrial Relations
Department of Business & Industry
1301 North Green Valley Parkway #200
Henderson, Nevada 89074
(702) 486-9159
Chief Admin. Officer
FAX: (702) 990-0362

New Hampshire
NH Department of Environmental Services
29 Hazen Drive-Post Office Box 95
Concord, New Hampshire 03302-0095
(603) 271-2024
21(d) Project Manager
FAX: (603) 271-2667

New Jersey
New Jersey Department of Labor
and Workforce Development
1 John Fitch Plaza
Post Office Box 386
Trenton, New Jersey 08625-0386
(609) 292-0501
Director
FAX: (609) 984-5706
(609) 984-0785
Project Manager
FAX: (609) 292-4409

New Mexico
New Mexico Environment Department
Occupational Health & Safety Bureau
525 Marquez Plaza
Santa Fe, New Mexico 87502
(505) 827-4230
Program Manager
FAX: (505) 827-4422

New York
Division of Safety and Health
State Office Building Campus
Building 12, Room 168
Albany, New York 12240
(518) 457-2238
Program Manager
FAX: (518) 457-3454

North Carolina
NC Department of Labor-OSHA Division
Bureau of Consultative Services
111 Hillsborough Street
Raleigh, North Carolina 27601

Mailing:
1101 Mail Service Center
Raleigh, North Carolina 27699-1101
(919) 807-2905
Bureau Chief
FAX: (919) 807-2902

North Dakota
ND Occupational Safety & Health Consultation-Bismarck
State College Corporate & Continuing Education
1815 Shaffer Street
Bismarck, North Dakota 58501

Mailing:
Post Office Box 5587
Bismarck, North Dakota 58506-5587
(701) 224-5778
Program Manager
FAX: (701) 224-5763

Northern Mariana Islands
Commonwealth of the Northern Mariana Islands (CNMI)
CNMI Department of Labor
CNMI-OSHA Consultation
Post Office Box 10007
2nd Floor-Afetnas Building, San Antonio
Saipan, MP 96950

Ohio
Bureau of Workers' Compensation
OSHA On-Site Consultation Program
13430 Yarmouth Drive
Pickerington, Ohio 43147
(670) 236-0989
Secretary of Labor
FAX: (670) 664-3158
(614) 466-7082
(800) 282-1425
Project Manager
FAX: (614) 644-3133

Oklahoma
Oklahoma Department of Labor
OSHA Division
4001 North Lincoln Boulevard
Oklahoma City, Oklahoma 73105-5212
(405) 528-1500 ext. 271
Director, OSHA Div.
FAX: (405) 557-1214

Oregon
Oregon OSHA Consultation/Services
Department of Consumer & Business
350 Winter Street, N.E., Room 430
Salem, Oregon 97301-3882
(503) 378-3272
Project Manager
FAX: (503) 947-7462

Pennsylvania
Indiana University of Pennsylvania
Walsh Hall-Room 210
302 East Walk
Indiana, Pennsylvania 15705-1087
(724) 357-2396
Project Manager
FAX: (724) 357-2385

Puerto Rico
PR Occupational Safety and Health Admin.
Dept. of Labor & Human Resources
21st Floor
505 Munoz Rivera Avenue
Hato Rey, Puerto Rico 00918
(787) 754-2171
Assistant Secretary
FAX: (787) 767-6051

Rhode Island
OSH Consultation Program
Div. of Occup. Health & Radiation Ctrl.
Rhode Island Department of Health
3 Capitol Hill, Cannon Bldg-Rm. 206
Providence, Rhode Island 02908
(401) 222-2438
Project Manager
FAX: (401) 222-2456

South Carolina
Office of OSHA Voluntary Programs
SC Department of Labor
Licensing & Regulation
110 Centerview Drive
P.O. Box 11329
Columbia, South Carolina 29211-1329
(803) 896-7744
Acting Administrator
FAX: (803) 896-7750

South Dakota
South Dakota State University
Engineering Extension, West Hall 118
Box 510
907 Harvey Dunn Street
Brookings, South Dakota 57007-0597
(605) 688-4101
Director
FAX: (605) 688-6290

Tennessee
OSHA Consultative Services Div.
Tennessee Department of Labor
Andrew Johnson Tower, 3rd Floor
710 James Robertson Parkway
Nashville, Tennessee 37243-0659
(615) 741-7155
Program Manager
FAX: (615) 532-2997

Texas
Texas Workers Compensation Commission
Workers Health and Safety Division
7551 Metro Center Drive-Suite 100
Austin, Texas 78744-1609
(512) 804-4640, (800) 687-7080
Project Manager
FAX: (512) 804-4641

OSHA
Occupational Safety and
Health Administration

Utah
State of Utah
OSHA Consultation Program
160 East 300 South, Third Floor
Salt Lake City, Utah 84114-6650
(801) 530-6855
Project Manager
FAX : (801) 530-6992

Vermont
Div. of Occupational Safety & Health
Vermont Dept. of Labor & Industry
National Life Building, Drawer #20
Montepilier, Vermont 05602-3401

Mailing:
Post Office Box 231
Hyde Park, Vermont 05655
(802) 888-0620
Project Director
FAX: (802) 888-2598

Virginia
VA Department of Labor & Industry
Occupational Safety and Health
Training and Consultation
13 South 13th Street
Powers-Taylor Building-Suite 319
Richmond, Virginia 23219
(804) 786-6613
Program Manager
FAX: (804) 786-8418
Director
FAX: (804) 786-6359

Virgin Islands
University of the Virgin Islands
Community Engagement & Lifelong Learning
#2 John Brewer's Bay
St. Thomas, Virgin Islands 00803
(340) 693-1101
Program Manager
FAX: (340) 693-1115

Washington
WA Department of Labor & Industries
WISHA Services Division
7273 Linderson Way, SW
Tumwater, Washington 98501-5414

Mailing:
Post Office Box 44640
Olympia, Washington 98504-4640
(360) 902-5554
Program Manager
FAX: (360) 902-5459

West Virginia
West Virginia Department of Labor
Capitol Complex Bldg #6, Room B-749
1800 East Washington Street
Charleston, West Virginia 25305
(304) 558-7890
Project Manager
FAX: (304) 558-2415

Wisconsin (Health)
WI OSHA Health Consultation Program
Wisconsin State Laboratory of Hygiene
Environmental Health Division
2601 Agriculture Drive
Madison, Wisconsin 53707-7996

Mailing:
Post Office Box 7996
Madison, Wisconsin 53707-7996
(608) 226-5239 or 40
Director
FAX: (608) 226-5249

Wisconsin (Safety)
Department of Commerce
Division of Safety & Buildings
WI Safety &Consultation Bureau
Southeast Regional State Office Building
141 NW Barstow Street
Waukesha, Wisconsin 53188-3789
(262) 521-5198
1-800-947-0553
Admin. Manager
FAX: (262) 521-5369

Wyoming
Wyoming Workers' Safety
1510 East Pershing Blvd.
Cheyenne, Wyoming 82002
(307) 777-7786
Program Manager
FAX: (307) 777-3646